RAINBOWS
FOR GOALPOSTS

RAINBOWS
FOR GOALPOSTS

A JOURNEY TO
THE HEART OF
THE WORLD CUP

RICHARD JONES

Published By:
Know The Score Books
Pitch Publishing (Brighton) Ltd
A2 Yeoman Gate
Yeoman Way
Durrington
BN13 3QZ

Email: info@pitchpublishing.co.uk
Web: www.pitchpublishing.co.uk

First published 2010

ISBN: 9781848185265

A catalogue record for this book is available from the British Library.

Typeset in Adobe Garamond Pro 11pt/14pt

Printed and bound in Malta by Gutenberg Press

For my family, English and African

CONTENTS

ACKNOWLEDGEMENTS

I AM DEEPLY GRATEFUL TO ALL THOSE WHO SHARED THEIR TIME, insights and experiences especially Moses, Nelly, Ronnie, Phumla, Colleen, Marcus, Lalas and Sydney.

I am also indebted to Richard and Andrea Starkey, Alison Bullen and the Dugmore family – Ron and Gill, Craig and Michelle, Cameron and Melanie, Cuan and Ann – for generously providing everything from food and shelter to match tickets.

I would also like to thank my agent James Wills at Watson, Little Ltd for his guidance and encouragement and all at Pitch Publishing for their enthusiasm in taking this project on.

Above all my thanks and love go to Tess, for sharing this journey with me.

The extract from *Chaos* by James Gleick, published by William Heinemann, is reprinted by permission of The Random House Group Ltd.

INTRODUCTION

IT IS A SWELTERING AFTERNOON IN THE KING ZWELITHINI Stadium on the outskirts of Durban and the crowd is baying like a playground mob. The Amazulu striker is teasing his marker – feint, shimmy, shibobo, tsamaya – urging an indiscretion. When the defender obliges he does so with gusto, felling his tormentor with a heartfelt boot up the backside. The burly matron sitting next to me rises and bustles along to the end of the concrete seating block, stopping in front of a policeman snoozing in the shade of the corrugated iron grandstand. She lifts a long, ivy-green, plastic trumpet to her lips and puckers up. Phoowarp! The lawman snorts into life, groping for the dark arsenal dangling from his belt. He squints up at the woman, a pained enquiry on his face. She waggles her vuvuzela towards the pitch indicating the guilty party – now raising his palms to the referee, a study in bemused innocence.

"Offeeca, I *hope* you are watching thees; I *expect* you to arrest that naughty boy!"

Hope and expectation – instantly recognisable sporting themes, grossly exaggerated in a World Cup year; they are also the twin dynamos driving the cultural and social evolutions of the host nation. For South Africa, staging one of the great sporting and media events offered the chance to repaint itself in the eyes of the world, to splash some colour across a canvas dulled by the heavy-handed, monochrome brush-strokes of the Apartheid years.

During the past decade I have been a regular visitor to the Republic – not as a reporter or correspondent – just travelling between my wife's family and friends, absorbing the sights and sounds of a unique, complex society. While these trips provided a flavour of the country,

I never truly felt that I had come close to unravelling the knotted threads of modern South African life. But in recent years watching the World Cup preparations unfold (and occasionally unravel) I began to see football, with its historical, cultural and inevitably racial undercurrents, as the ideal map by which to navigate this fascinating, beautiful landscape. I travelled the country before the tournament, watching games and talking to fans and others involved at different levels of the game, before returning to see the greatest show on earth make its debut on African soil.

I hoped that this journey around an alien football culture might help me to better understand where I now find myself in relation to my own. We are back to hope and expectation. There I am in 1982, a ten-year-old kneeling in silent prayer before the TV, watching through my fingers as Bryan Robson scoops the ball from the by-line into the Spanish penalty area. England's number seven awaits its arrival – a diminutive, luxuriously-permed saviour; a playground deity: Jesus saves, but Keegan scores the rebound. Not this time. The ball springs off his bubbly helmet and loops wide of the post. The whistle blows, England are out of the World Cup: I feel my lower lip start to wobble and soon after, the tears roll. The stiff upper lip four years later hid gritted teeth, marvelling at the dark genius of Maradona. In 1990 when Chris Waddle scooped his penalty high into the night sky over Turin my heart slid quietly down my trouser leg. The tournament had been so engaging, the sense of loss when it ended was palpable and lasting. But 16 years later, when Cristiano Ronaldo sent us packing from Germany in 2006, I just sighed and flicked over to catch the last ten minutes of *Bargain Hunt*.

Two decades on from Italia '90, watching Fabio's men march purposefully towards Africa I felt strangely detached, almost ambivalent. Why? As the Premier League and Champions League have gathered riches, glamour and success, the international scene seems to have lost its sparkle. The consequent over-selling probably doesn't help – "When we come back, the whole game exclusively live, strap yourself in folks, it's England v Andorra, from Portman Road…" A large part of the answer, I suspect, lies in the fact that the chasm separating players and fans is fast becoming a canyon. Unimaginable wages, Bentleys and Hummers, tattoos and bling, Cristal waterfalls at Boujis and Mahiki, WAGs akimbo, occasional slippage into the third person during interviews. Who are these people? Do we like them? (not always) Do we envy them? (a little) Are we still on their side? (discuss). In recent seasons England crowds have become accustomed to booing England players.

As for England's prospects, I was tempted to side with Gazza – "I don't make predictions, and I never will" – but I couldn't suppress a nagging feeling that the time was right for a half-decent showing. I arrived at this view privately, personally – several months before the tabloid storm broke, showering us with pun-soaked predictions, drenching us in national fervour. Ahead of the tournament, watching the flags of St George appear on cars and houses, listening to the gentle hiss of the tabloid hyperbole bubble expanding fit to burst, I had to hope that the eventual outcome would arrest the growing divide between England players and their fans.

While it's easy to catalogue what's been gained by English football since 1990 – 'the Big Four', prawn sandwiches, simulation, the need for a Respect Campaign – pinning down what has been lost often proves more difficult. Until I remember that afternoon in the King Zwelithini Stadium.

The woman shuffled back along our row and retook her place, releasing a mournful sigh as her buttocks were reunited with the unforgiving concrete step.

"Ag man, sometimes you must do these theengs," she announced. "If we don't have a nice game eet will be lost – you will lose *eet*."

"Lose what?" I asked.

She tapped a clenched fist on her chest and leant close to share a husky stage whisper, "Inhliziyo, *Inh-li-ziyo*. The heart."

Well, it was a start.

SCREAMER

IN 2006, AS PART OF THEIR QUINQUAGENARY CELEBRATIONS,
the Confederation of African Football asked its membership to
nominate the best players of the last fifty years. Second and third
spots were occupied by Mahmoud El Khatib and Hossam Hassan.
No? OK, try another: a man called Roger topped the list. Now
you're nodding and smiling. Now you can see the broad grin
spreading beneath a neat moustache, the flash of green and red, the
snaky hips seducing the corner flag. Now you can see Roger Milla,
the man who outshone Diego, Toto, even Gazza at Italia '90 and in
doing so symbolised the sudden arrival of African football on the
world stage.

The opening game of the tournament pitted Cameroon against
the holders, Argentina. Despite being reduced to ten men early in
the second half, the underdogs clung tenaciously to a one-goal lead;
frustration creased the rotund countenance of El Pibe de Oro, and
my heart filled with love for the Indomitable Lions. By the time
the colossal Benjamin Massing had booted a goal-bound Claudio
Caniggia into the stand, I was besotted. The sky blue and white
stripes still evoked painful memories of England's last World Cup
exit, slapped round the chops by the hand of God. I'm ashamed
to say that as big Ben's boot disappeared up Caniggia's backside
I cheered it home. Deep in a shadowy corner of my soul, a moral
wasteland littered with the balled-up remnants of tabloid bile, I
heard myself mutter: "Go on son, give him one from me." I take no
pride in that admission, but it's said now, so let's not dwell on it.

Twenty years on, the World Cup's opening game again set Africa
against South America, and if the sights and sounds within Soccer

City were anything to go by, another memorable month of football lay ahead. The crowd was a seething mass of noise and colour – the bright yellow shirts of Bafana Bafana complemented by the blues, reds and greens of many thousand rainbow nation flags. One way or another in South Africa colour seems inescapable. It is colour that seduces visitors into the country – the Persil-white tablecloth spreading across Cape Town's famous peak, the gilded grasslands of the game parks, the fresh pastels of Bo-Kaap, the turquoise surf of the Durban beachfront – drawing the eye away from the long shadows of the past. The flag, bringing together the colours of the previously divided groups, is an eye-catching emblem of unity.

From a distance it is easy, or perhaps just more comfortable, to believe that the disease that Apartheid spread across the country cured itself the day that Nelson Mandela walked out of the Victor Verster Prison in February 1990. Of course this is not the case. The Apartheid Museum in Johannesburg leads visitors on a journey through the design, development and ultimate demise of this crass experiment in social engineering. As you near the exit the walls are filled with the joyous, colourful scenes that accompanied the assembly of the new parliament. Amongst these a monochrome photograph taken shortly after the landmark elections of 1994 captures a group of whites in Pretoria gleefully igniting their new national flag.

Two years after those first elections, Soccer City witnessed a defining moment for South African football. In 1996, a year in which England came perilously close to winning an international tournament on home soil, Bafana Bafana went one better. The Boys coasted into the latter stages of that year's African Nations Cup on a wave of momentum built by expectant local support. Thirty thousand fans turned up to the FNB – a towering citadel on the edge of the Soweto Highway – to see goals from Mark Fish and John 'Shoes' Moshoeu dispose of the Algerians. The crowd had swollen to 70,000 for the semi-final against Ghana – a significant landmark on the African football map, harbouring the threat posed by Abédi Pelé, the aptly-named star of the great Olympique Marseilles team of the early 1990s.

The hordes chanting for Bafana had icons of their own; "Feeeesh!" went the cry as a long, silvery snoek was hoisted and passed above their heads. For "Shoes" the "ooh" vowel-sound stretched into a moan of collective reverence; "Shooooe-sssss" hissed around Soccer City as he booted the Ghanaians aside with a brace of goals. The official record tells us that 80,000 fans filled the FNB for the final; township legend places the figure closer to 140,000. Health and safety took a back seat: walls were scaled, fences breached, everyone breathed in. And then out again 90 minutes later as a tumult of noise welcomed a 2-0 victory over Tunisia.

A year earlier, across town at Ellis Park, Francois Pienaar, a strapping, blonde Afrikaaner, had accepted the rugby World Cup from a beaming Nelson Mandela, both men wearing the dark green Springbok jersey. For many this was a defining tableau for the new South Africa. When Madiba (the honorary title bestowed on Mandela) handed Neil Tovey the African Nations Cup the following year, it seemed that Bafana were ready to follow their counterparts from the rugby world on to the global stage. However, as with the English side, it would soon become apparent that 1996 was just a glimpse of the summit, before a tumble back down towards the foothills.

Two seasons later in Burkina Faso, the Boys reached another Nations Cup final, but this time lost to Egypt. In the same year a World Cup debut came and went in France – friends were made, but few headlines. Four years later they reappeared in the first Asian World Cup, but departed early in a tournament in which the pop-guns blew away many of the big shots. The team failed to reach the finals in Germany in 2006, after limping out of the African championship earlier that year without a single goal to their name. Bafana did not appear at the 2010 African finals in Angola, having been eliminated by their old nemesis Nigeria.

This failure to build on their triumph in 1996 has enhanced the standing of rugby as the dominant feature of the South African sporting landscape. The men chasing the egg are double world champions that hold their own in the Tri-nations and Super 14 tournaments – a success story in a hemisphere that views second place as first loser.

Against this backdrop it is unsurprising that many in South Africa were fretting over the fortunes of the national team at their own World Cup. There is a tradition of unfancied host nations rising to the occasion: Sweden in 1958, Chile in 1962, Mexico in 1986, the US in 1994, Japan and South Korea in 2002. As I travelled the country talking to fans before the big kick-off, there were many that doubted whether Bafana were capable of repeating this trick. The local support had a mixed-up feel. Some seemed determined to resist engagement, waiting for the Super 14 to restart the serious sporting business. Others were looking forward to seeing some top-flight football from the South Americans and Europeans, but remained ambivalent about the home nation. Closer to the heart of the football community there was more hope than expectation, tempered by strong allegiances to their clubs. Finally, a hefty core contingent was clearly determined to follow Bafana, cheering, honking vuvuzelas, willing them forward into a prolonged adventure. It struck me that if the team could defy form and exceed expectations, dragging all these groups, like it or not, into a prolonged adventure, unifying a sports-mad nation for a week or even a few days, it would represent a rare and precious victory that would dwarf that of the eventual winner.

Starting proceedings in Jo'burg was a smart move. In Soweto, at the heart of the South African football community, inspiration could be drawn from the heroes of the past. Prior to kick-off the camera panned around the stadium, picking out the grandees of the domestic game; legends on the lookout for a new generation of stars.

There was the round, cheerful face of Kaizer Motaung, a king in his court. His team, the Kaizer Chiefs, were born out of a gradual, sometimes violent, process of dismantling the order established within the Johannesburg football community. Matters came to a head in 1969 over proposals to stage a one-off 'championship decider' between Orlando Pirates, the leading African side, and Highlands Park, the pre-eminent team from the exclusively white league. The plans led to unrest within the Pirates camp and the eventual expulsion of three dissenting players. The rebels were approached by Kaizer, a young Pirates striker making a name for himself with Atlanta Chiefs during a fleeting bubble of interest in 'soccer' in the States. Kaizer's XI, as they were originally known, rejected the rigid traditions and fanaticism of the existing clubs, eschewing the violence that often marred local matches. They adopted the slogan 'love and peace' and a style – flares, beads, afro hairstyles – lifted from the culture that Motaung had seen developing in America. Their playing strip, in stark contrast to the all black/skull and crossbones of the Pirates kit, radiated gold, and their club badge depicted the calm, distinguished profile of a Native American chief.

In 1971, when South African Breweries sponsored a professional tournament for African clubs in the shape of the delightful-sounding Keg League, the Amakhosi ('chiefs' in Zulu) entered the fray. The Chiefs were rebels and they looked arrestingly cool; qualities guaranteed to ensnare the devotion of the South African football-watching public. Happily, they could play a bit too. Throughout the seventies and eighties this renegade outfit, with branding borrowed from an alien culture, rose steadily to the summit of the game, dragging the hearts and minds of a growing legion of followers with them.

Their fame has even spread to England, albeit by a rather circuitous route. In 1994 Lucas Radebe, then a leading Chiefs player, signed for Leeds United – re-treading a trail blazed by his

countrymen Gerry Francis and Albert Johanneson at the turn of
the sixties. Radebe spent over a decade in Yorkshire during which
time Leeds scaled heights not reached since their domination of
English football in the 1970s. The last club to win the old league
championship, they would become the first high-profile casualty of
the boom or bust world of the new Premier League. The handsome,
totemic figure, marshalling their defence with a muscular grace,
soon became a terrace idol. In fact one group of young men were so
smitten they named their band in his honour.

And then there's Jomo Sono – a legend from across town, the
other mob: Orlando Pirates. The first time I laid eyes on Jomo, about
a decade ago in Cape Town, he was using the kind of chair you
would normally find stacked against the wall of a primary school
gym as an umbrella. Storm clouds had rolled in from the ocean,
glanced off Table Mountain and sent a deluge in the direction
of the Athlone Stadium, a small ground sitting between the city
suburbs and the squalid sprawl of the Cape Flats. As a player Sono,
like Kaizer Motaung before him, travelled to the States to try his
luck in the North American Soccer League, lining up alongside
the likes of Pelé, Franz Beckenbauer and Carlos Alberto in the
legendary New York Cosmos side. When he returned to South
Africa in 1982, Jomo – who had originally followed the footsteps
of his late father Eric 'Scara' Sono into the Pirates elite – created
his own football brand, taking over the ailing Highlands Park club
to form Jomo Cosmos. Within five years they had won the league,
within another five they lifted the splendid-sounding Bobsave
Superbowl. A lively, tricky player with a lethal curling delivery, it
is Sono's coaching credentials that place him at the centre of the
South African footballing establishment. The rather stout figure
that I watched stalking the touchline with a plastic chair on his
head that sodden night at Athlone was the technical brains behind
the Bafana Bafana victory in the African Nations Cup of 1996.
Two years later he almost repeated the trick, when parachuted into

the coach's hot seat at the eleventh hour following the sacking of 'The White Witchdoctor', Philippe Troussier.

The fanatical devotion to Chiefs and Pirates lies at the heart of South African football and I wondered where this left Bafana Bafana. Before the tournament I spoke to Luke Alfred, a Johannesburg-based journalist, about Bafana's chances; he identified the gap between passionate local knowledge and international smarts.

"It's all Gauteng-centric: Chiefs and Pirates, maybe [Mamdelodi] Sundowns. Beyond that you really only find fanaticism out in Bloem with Celtic. Essentially you have a game which is passionate, but parochial. We're geographically isolated here, with little prospect of lively competition from our near neighbours. This sense of separation tends to focus attention on the local big guns, which to an extent fuels an inflated sense of their value. Outside South Africa, Chiefs and Pirates would struggle to make an impression, but here there seems to be a cherished myth that they could live with anyone: it's the triumph of legend over reality – look at Jomo, this revered tactician has no coaching badges, just his reputation.

"South African football has a dangerous over-reliance on the notion that things will come good – even without proper coaching or administration. Look at the youth programme. In the 15 years since our readmission we have sent only one side to the World Youth Championships. And yet still the question is asked: where are the next Bafana stars coming from?"

The current stars were singing and dancing as they followed their skipper, Aaron Mokoena, down the tunnel. Unlike many of his charges, the veteran of over 100 international matches could at least draw on experiences from the wider world of football. Blackburn, Portsmouth, Genk might not have quite the same ring as London, Paris, Milan but the skipper's CV bore evidence of a knowledge of football beyond the hotbeds of Gauteng. When Mokoena left South Africa to pursue a career abroad, like the previous skipper Lucas Radebe, he bore scars of the harsh realties of life back home;

bullets flying in the township, both men narrowly cheated death. This kind of life experience no doubt gives a sportsman a heightened sense of perspective, a clearer idea of where chasing a ball around a field fits into the grander scheme. Even then, as Mokoena led his boys out at Soccer City, the outward show of cheerful intent must have masked a ton of pressure. The expectation was intense. You only had to listen to the vuvuzelas to realise that.

A metre-long, plastic tube finishing in a trumpeting funnel, a vuvuzela resembles the kind of slender clarion used to sound a royal fanfare in medieval times. In reality the noise they produce is anything but regal. I have heard their output likened to the sound of a charging elephant. Less romantically, it is perhaps better described as the sound one might involuntarily produce if faced with a charging elephant.

As the old saying goes: where there's a plastic trumpet that sounds like a flatulent rhino letting rip into an old tin bucket, there's brass. In 2001 a young entrepreneur called Neil van Schalkwyk won a youth enterprise scheme run by South African Breweries. With SAB's support, his fledgling company Masincedane Sport set about turning this curiosity into a mass-produced must-have for any discerning fan. Soon club-branded vuvuzelas were on sale at every ground. Twenty thousand were sold on the day Sepp Blatter confirmed that South Africa would host the 2010 World Cup. Having inadvertently given with one hand, it seemed for a while that Fifa would take back with the other. Deep within the bowels of its Zurich headquarters a committee of joyless souls had worked themselves into a pernickety lather about the presence of these blaring horns at their tournament. Someone from marketing popped their head around the door and soon all was well again. As long as they did not carry logos bearing branding from unofficial sponsors, no problem. Unfortunately the marketing guy left the door open, allowing someone from risk management to nip in. What if these long tubes were deployed as weapons? No one wants to be bludgeoned insensible with a plastic trumpet, right? Much head scratching later, the plan was set: Fifa would sanction the use of vuvuzelas in and around the 2010 stadia, having first advised the manufacturers to make them no heavier than 100g.

Shortly after the tournament began the debate was reopened when it became clear that the World Cup mood music was not to everyone's taste. Broadcasters fretted about sound quality, players were being blasted out of their comfort zone. Not long after his side's dismal goalless opener against Uruguay, France skipper Patrice Evra had already had enough. "We can't sleep at night because of the vuvuzelas. People start playing them from 6am. We can't hear one another out on the pitch because of them."

Sepp Blatter took a stand, blowing the trumpet for cultural diversity. Vuvuzelas are part of African football – we're playing football in Africa, deal with it.

As the South African and Mexican players stepped onto the turf, battle was joined in the stands: The Tijuana Brass -v- The Soweto Horn Section: no contest. The vuvuzelas raised a wall of sound – an endless, fruity Bronx cheer sharpened by the nagging buzz of a swarm of enraged hornets.

The speeches by Sepp Blatter and Jacob Zuma before kick-off shared an underlying theme; a major triumph had been achieved before a ball was kicked – the World Cup had finally arrived in Africa; South Africa had delivered it safely. But despite the victorious tone, there was still a match to be played. Wonderful though it was, the euphoric build-up left both sets of players with a fine line to tread between heroism and villainy.

For much of the first half the magnitude of the occasion was evident in Bafana's play: they looked unsure, tentative. Suddenly the romantic story that had been building for weeks was being sullied by the heartless reality of statistics: 60-odd Fifa ranking places separated the two sides, and it showed. The Mexicans settled swiftly into a neat, rhythmic passing game and were threatening to poop the party. On more than one occasion the home keeper – Chiefs' Itumeleng Khune – was called upon to keep his side on level terms. When 'El Tri' did finally get the ball in the net, a luxuriously complicated variation of the offside rule saved the day.

Not long after, during a skirmish on the edge of the penalty area, either by luck or design a Bafana defender shepherded the ball to safety by knocking it between the ankles of an onrushing forward. The volume of the vuvuzelas rose to 11, the tension lifted a few inches, a ripple of joy swept through the crowd. Shibobo!

Blurted out in flat British tones, 'nutmeg' has a functional sound to it; now try 'shibobo'. I dare you to tell me that you don't feel appreciably happier about life for having just bounced those three, cheeky syllables off your tongue. It's the sound that a Laughing Dove makes, its faintly mocking tone ringing from the tall branches of a milkwood tree. More than just the name of a trick, the word has become synonymous with the colour and joy of South African football. To celebrate Bafana's first World Cup adventure, the group TKZee recorded a single called *Shibobo* to send the boys on their way to France '98. It became the fastest-selling CD single in South African history. The opening is unpromising – a sample from *The Final Countdown*, the melodramatic anthem from 1980s perm-rockers Europe – but things improve rapidly. A heavy bass-line slides in over some breakbeats, Bafana legend Benni McCarthy starts rapping, and there's even a few "let's get ready to rumbles" thrown in. Tears ran down cheeks when *Nkosi Sikelel' iAfrika*, the joint national anthem since 1994, was sung before the 2010 kick-off; *Shibobo* is the anthem to get the crowd jumping. It's a song that reawakens happy memories of the days when Bafana took to the field more in expectation than hope. MadameQueen79's YouTube tribute says it all: "omg I love this song, my boyf even used to call me shibobo". The mind boggles.

It is hard to underestimate the importance placed on skill in South African football culture. Looking on in dismay at Bafana's lean run, many fans still eulogise about the great players of the past, winning with style, flair and a glut of shibobos – many of them emanating from the boot of the legendary Doctor Khumalo. Theophilus 'Doctor' Khumalo was a central figure in the success enjoyed by Kaizer Chiefs during the 1980s and 90s and played a key role in the Bafana Bafana side that lifted the African Cup of Nations in 1996. To many he now seems to represent a dim light glowing in a halcyon past, many bemoaning the day the Doctor left his shibobo surgery for the final time.

If Chiefs fans loved Doctor Khumalo for his shibobos, they harboured a similar affection for Thabo Mooki and his tsamayas. A no-nonsense drag-back in the British vernacular suddenly enters romantic new territory: "Tsamaya!" – you can almost hear the victorious hoots from the crowd as the player teases the defenders. Mooki turned the tsamaya into an art form; his *tsiki-tsiki* ('shaky-shaky') dribbles and feints left defenders standing and the golden hordes in the stands baying for more. Another favourite with the Amakhosi faithful, Isaac 'Shakes' Kungwane inadvertently penned a new entry in the register of *Diski* slang during a match against local rivals Moroka Swallows. Approaching goal with the ball at his feet, Kungwane steadied himself for a ferocious shot at goal. Fearing a punt in the face, or worse, the Swallows defender Lucky Molefe turned his back, at which point Kungwane dropped his shoulder and trotted merrily on his way. The 'show me your number' was born that day.

I remember gaping in awe the first time I saw Roberto Baggio wrong-foot a defender by chipping the ball into the box, from behind his standing leg. I have since been assured that Mlungiji 'Professor' Ngubane, a star player with the Durban Bush Bucks in the 1970s and 80s, was way ahead of Il Divin Codino with that one.

This appetite for the garnish over the meat means that in South Africa football is not to everyone's taste. For rugby and cricket followers – broadly speaking a white, middle-class audience – football is a game of tricks and nonsense, no substance, no end product. By contrast, for the football fans I have spoken to, skills and flamboyance lie at the heart of their love for the game – they adore the shibobos and tsamayas. Faced with a more direct, pragmatic approach introduced by imported coaches, the playing style is dismissed as charmless, in Afrikaans 'skop en donder' - kick and run.

The referee blew for half-time and the Bafana coach headed off down the tunnel to share a few well-chosen words with his players. Time to earn his corn. Having steered Brazil to their fourth World Cup title in 1994, Carlos Alberto Parreira embarked on a footballing odyssey that took in Spain, Turkey, New York and Saudi Arabia. At the start of 2007 he washed up in South Africa, touted by the South African Football Association (SAFA) as the man to lead Bafana to glory in 2010. But there were problems. Firstly, his new employers had forgotten to apply for a work permit. Once permitted to work he could reasonably expect payment, and that was the second problem. When the South African Broadcasting Corporation broke the news that Parreira was on R1.8m (about £150,000) per month, the storm broke. In England we have long-since become hardened to the Monopoly money wafted in front of football's elite, but in South Africa this was news. Former Bafana player and goalkeeping coach Roger De Sá – a veteran of the 1996 Nations Cup triumph – described the salary as "shocking, sickening and obscene".

To put the figure into some sort of context, the average monthly wage of a worker in the 'formal' business sector at that time was about R7,000. And that doesn't account for the pittances earned within the vast 'informal' work sector – the township traders, the guys you see in their blue overalls piled in the back of bakkies heading for work in the fields. In short, the kind of people that love football and can find R20 to go and see a game, but maybe not R40 to buy a seat in the shade. And then there was Benni McCarthy. Parreira was looking to the future, blooding youth; there was no place for Bafana's brightest star and leading scorer in his plans.

The Brazilian's stay was brief – it began and finished with 3-0 victories, the latter ironically featuring a goal from the recalled McCarthy. Just over a year after arriving, Parreira was on his way. His explanation that he wanted to be with his sick wife did not stop the rumour mill grinding out a few gritty morsels about failed relationships with the SAFA hierarchy and a fresh 2010 panic for the media to sink their teeth into.

The media storm that followed Parreira's sudden departure blew harder when the news of his replacement broke. It is ironic that a country whose football culture prizes style and flair chose successive managers from the birthplace of the beautiful game that earned their spurs by winning ugly. Parreira's replacement, Joel Santana, was a familiar name in Brazilian football having managed each of the four major clubs – Botafogo, Flamengo, Fluminense and Vasco da Gama – but he was largely unknown in the wider world. His defensive ethos was put to an immediate test with a trip to Nigeria for an African Nations Cup qualifier. The home and away fixtures with the Super Eagles would determine whether South Africa would appear in Angola 2010 as a prelude to their own World Cup later that year. A narrow defeat in Abuja swung the spotlight on to the return leg in Port Elizabeth; Santana's men needed to win to preserve their Nations Cup hopes. Playing at an old rugby venue deemed unfit for league football Bafana lost the game 0-1, and with it their chances of appearing in the African championship. There were whispers about a new coach; SAFA backed their man.

A strong showing by Bafana six months later in the Confederations Cup – their tenacity against the Brazilians was a notable highlight – boosted Santana's campaign to silence the critics. But a subsequent run of defeats against Serbia, Germany, the Republic of Ireland, Norway and Iceland, broken only by a

1-0 win over Madagascar, plunged Bafana back into crisis. With only seven months to go before the World Cup, decisive action was needed. Santana was ushered through the back door marked 'by mutual consent', allowing SAFA to replace him with a man who offered not only a proven World Cup pedigree but also familiarity with South African football. His name? Carlos Alberto Parreira.

Despite this chaotic, often farcical courtship, the relationship between the Brazilian and Bafana Bafana had started to blossom as the World Cup countdown hit single figures. A dozen games unbeaten was the kind of form to inspire genuine belief amongst the fans. Whatever Parreira said at half-time, when his boys lined up against the Mexicans for the second half, they clearly had some too. Buckets of it.

Suddenly there were crisp passes zipping between the backline and midfield, setting up incisive thrusts down the forward channels. Suddenly Bafana were showing some attacking threat as their pacy, darting runners bore down on the Mexican rearguard. Teko Modise and Siphiwe Tshabalala led the way and the vuvuzelas whined with joy. Here was a Pirates/Chiefs double-act taking on the world without fear, a stone's throw from the endless sprawl of Soweto. Here was South African football showing its true colours. Just before the hour mark a lightning fast one-touch move set Tshabalala away down the left with a half-decent sight of the Mexican goal. Watching the swish of his dreadlocks I felt a sudden surge of recognition. Hello, I thought, it's screamer.

This sense of déjà vu dragged me back a year or so to a golden Sunday afternoon in Orkney, a small town up in the mining heartlands north of Johannesburg. A crumbling old behemoth, the Oppenheimer Stadium was a world away from the modern masterpiece then under construction in Soccer City. The earthy brown stadium rose from the flatlands; the only other features breaking the horizon were grassy heaps of excavated earth and the rusting spokes of winding towers. It felt like a portal to the past, providing a glimpse of the origins of South African football. It was here, in this deceptively fruitful landscape, decades earlier, that the seeds of football in Gauteng were sown, as groups of mineworkers organised themselves first into teams and then leagues.

From all directions fans drifted across the fields, drawn by the buzz of the match. As a nod to the roots of football in the region a number of them sported mining hardhats, their usually functional appearance transformed by stripping away the toughened outer shell and teasing the shards of plastic into beautifully jagged sculptures.

We rushed past vendors offering sizzling legs of chicken, blocks of frozen watermelon and cigarettes, paid R20 to the ticket steward and climbed to a vantage point on the curved corner at the top of the uncovered seating block. I leant against a rusting rail – a pipe supplying drinking water to a network of taps around the ground, which juddered gently in the small of my back when used. The familiar smell of dagga, South African cannabis, drifted across the crowd and mingled with the smoke wafting up at us from the braai grills outside the ground. On all sides a forest of vuvuzelas blasted out a rhythmic honk complemented by the occasional rise and fall of an air-raid siren.

Chiefs were taking on Cosmos. Far below us on the touchline the portly figure of Jomo Sono paced anxiously, sweating under a red baseball cap, like a middle-manager at KFC fire-fighting his way through a busy lunchtime rush. Further down the line the mood of his Turkish counterpart, Muhsin Ertuğral, swung between the shipping lanes of the Bosphorus – a European shrug of exasperated indifference here, a flash of Ottoman rage there.

The match was a tight ball of tension, devoid of quality – an energetic but unstructured stalemate with both sides looking to improve upon an indifferent start to the season. Fearful of defeat, too scared to push for victory. A Chiefs attack built ponderously, another reckless shot rose to meet us at the top of the stand; the referee put the first half out of its misery and Moses – friend, lifelong Chiefs fan, eternal pessimist – let out an exasperated "Eish, man, useless!" and skulked off to get us some drinks.

Shortly after he left, on the opposite side of the ground I spotted a knot of fans gathering on the running track separating the stands from the pitch. They looked strangely incongruous, and it was only when the knot unravelled into a more disparate mob that I realised why. They were dressed in black: Pirates fans. The group began a slow procession around the track. At their head a tall figure in ebony priest's robes sporting a lank wig of white bangs and a tufty white stick-on beard and brandishing a bible with vaudevillian flourishes, led the chanting, swaying rabble behind him. Orkney was a long enough way to come to watch your own team; why had these guys made the trip? The answer was simple. Pirates were sitting pretty, near the summit of the league, Chiefs were languishing many places below – the former had simply sent a delegation to let the latter know all about it; these boys were on a *Schadenfreude* away-day.

The crowd had been simmering gently for some time, railing against the keystone antics of their players on the pitch. The sight of Reverend Wind-up and his flock seemed to turn exasperation into anger. Soon enough a rival group of Chiefs fans had gathered on the track and begun to march. I recognised instantly the man leading them. Saddam Maake – the Chiefs' celebrated Number One Fan – was unmistakable in his trademark comically-oversized glasses and No15 Khumalo shirt. As the two factions advanced towards each other the crowd bayed encouragingly.

The piratical pastor and his men were getting into their stride, raising the odds: a laconic shuffle became a briskly metronomic routine: step-step-jump, step-step-jump. Seized by a rising sense of panic and blessed with supreme ignorance I viewed this as some sort of Zulu-style war dance; a prelude to battle. The Chiefs contingent responded in kind, reforming their group into a tighter phalanx and quickening the pace. The crowd soon picked up the new beat with their vuvuzelas – tooting rhythmic parps of encouragement at the Chiefs, blasting elongated raspberries at the Pirates. Suddenly, I presume on a signal from Maake, the Chiefs army raised its battle insignia – anything and everything gold and black was waved in the air: flags, banners, umbrellas, shirts, mining helmets. At one point, as God is my witness, a colossal Sooty appeared above the mob, bristling with cuddly defiance, shaken by some unseen hand. By now there was less than ten metres of the rough, terracotta running track separating the two groups. My mind raced. What if the inferno of violence that was clearly about to explode spread to the stands? Where would that leave me? Sticking out like a sore, Caucasian thumb – a sitting target for an angry mob eager to get decades of antipathy towards whites out of their collective system by pummelling it into mine. A man advanced towards me brandishing a bottle.

"Eish, these guys."

I took the icy Coke from Moses and tried to match his insouciance.

"What's going to happen?" I trilled in a nonchalant falsetto.

"Let's see."

Below us Maake and the priest were face to face. The latter waggled his bible, the former peered over his vast spectacles disdainfully. Seconds passed like hours. And then it erupted – a riot of singing, dancing, flag-waving and hooting; Sooty popped up again, now bouncing happily on the shoulders of a Pirates fan, both bereft of their former aggression. This was not the ugly farrago I had anticipated, rather a joyful fiesta celebrating the collective supremacy of the two clubs that mattered most in the land. I asked Moses if this was normal.

"These days things are OK, but maybe ten years ago, eish it was still bad. When Chiefs played Pirates, trouble followed – naughty times."

He gestured towards the far side of the ground with his Coke bottle.

"Sometimes you would see fighting and then a body gets thrown over the side, falling like a sack of potatoes."

At the Orkney stadium in January 1991, this 'naughtiness' between Chiefs and Pirates fans claimed the lives of 43 fans, most of them trampled or crushed as panic spread following fighting in the stands. And that was during a pre-season *friendly*. Thankfully, it seems that in recent times the love and peace ethos espoused at the birth of Chiefs has returned. It is not immediately apparent why the fans chose love over war but corporate intervention may be part of the answer. Since Vodacom took on the sponsorship of both sides, the telecommunications giant has involved the players and fans in bipartite community projects in the poorer, football-mad areas of Johannesburg. This togetherness has also opened up lucrative windows onto the wider world of football, with Manchester United and Tottenham Hotspur visiting Gauteng for pre-season fixtures in the Vodacom Challenge. This marriage of football and commerce is further evidenced by the appearance of Pirates in the South African edition of the *Superbrands* directory. Here the Bucs stand shoulder to shoulder with corporate heavyweights like Coca-Cola, Microsoft and King Pie. "The product is soccer, but the service is entertainment", explains their entry, boiling down decades of passion, love, hatred, sacrifice, hope and despair into a gruel-thin, corporate sound bite.

The match was drifting towards a goalless conclusion when a pass of rare quality from the Chiefs' left-back incised the advancing Cosmos midfield and found a colleague standing idle in the centre circle. The man who took possession of the ball had more reason than most to use it wisely. Kaizer Motaung Junior, the son of the club owner, advanced cautiously up the right flank before scooping a delightful pass to the edge of the Cosmos box. The ball dropped at the feet of the Chiefs' No14, Siphiwe Tshabalala; he took a sighter and let fly. The contact was true, the ball shot past the static keeper, and flew like an arrow straight into the top right-hand corner of the stand, upending the Coke that Moses had left at his feet. It had been half full, now it was half empty. "Eish."

Easy to pick out with his flailing dreads, Tshabalala had been the target of heckling for some time; all around us his contributions were increasingly greeted with a nasally groaned chorus of "Screamer! Screamer!" Seeing my blank expression, Moses explained that this was a mocking reference to his namesake, Stanley 'Screamer' Tshabalala, a coach known in South African football circles as a partially-sighted visionary, marooned somewhere between tactical genius and nutcase. His preferred playing style, known as 'piano and shoeshine' (or *tiki tiki*), relied on baffling the opposition with a high-speed pass and move game, overlaid with teasing trickery. The style had reached its zenith in the late eighties when Screamer's Mamelodi Sundowns team had broken up the Chiefs/Pirates monopoly in the top flight.

Siphiwe Tshabalala was brought off soon after his wild shot and trudged off the field to derisive hoots. I watched him walk slowly to the line then cast a glance over my shoulder at the miles of dusty wilderness all around. I felt for him – a young man trying to make an impression, booed off in a dull game in the middle of nowhere.

The feeling amongst South Africa's football cognoscenti ahead of the 2010 kick-off seemed to be that Parreira was close to achieving a balance between Bafana's instinctive urge to entertain and the need for an end product. *Tiki tiki* but with a sharpened point. The wonderfully fluid move on the hour mark of their game against Mexico bore this out. There was Tshabalala wide on the left – pretty much where I'd left him at Orkney some 18 months earlier – collecting the final pass. The ball dropped at the feet of Bafana Bafana's No8; he took a sighter and let fly. The contact was true, the ball shot past the static keeper, and flew like an arrow straight into the top right-hand corner of the net, upending the form book.

Tshabalala, Modise, Reneilwe Letsholonyane and Kagisho Dikgacoi raced to the touchline and performed a carefully rehearsed rain dance. More than just a spontaneous outpouring of joy, their routine earned the Replenish Africa Initiative (RAIN) – a charity sponsored by Coca-Cola – $1,500 to put towards sanitation programmes aimed at curbing the spread of disease in schools across Africa. Bill Shankly famously asserted that football was more serious than life and death. Who knows, maybe that goal will prove to be a lifesaver.

It certainly changed Siphiwe Tshabalala's life that day. A sorry figure when I last saw him, he was now on top of the world, the newly-elected mayor of Soccer City. He had just scored the first goal of the first African World Cup and it was a screamer, an absolute screamer.

HOWLER

When England lost a crucial World Cup qualifier to the Dutch in 1993, on a dismal night in Rotterdam, the reaction of their manager said it all: "Do I not like that." Graham Taylor's howl of indignation, captured by a film crew documenting his team's failure to qualify for USA '94, confirmed the worst fears of England's supporters. If the gaffer struggled to arrange a five-word sentence into the correct order, what hope for the 11 bodies he was shuffling desperately between 4-4-2 and 4-2-4 formations? Not much. The match bore the twin hallmarks of a classic English footballing disaster: perceived injustice, palpable ineptitude.

David Platt got the ball rolling in the 56th minute, coaxing the Dutch sweeper into hauling him down into the penalty area. The German referee, Karl-Josef Assenmacher, awarded a free kick, waving away English cries for a penalty – correctly, the foul had occurred just outside the box – and crucially ignoring pleas to dismiss the last defender for a professional foul. So much for the slings and arrows, now for the custard pie. Within a few minutes the Dutch had secured a free kick of their own, 30 yards out from the English goal. Enter stage left Ronald Koeman, one of the world's leading executioners of a dead ball.

The art of positioning a defensive wall has a faint whiff of mathematics about it. The goalkeeper needs to calculate velocity, distance, angles and the potential for curvature in the ball's trajectory. Only then can he line up a row of men, nervously cupping their crown jewels. Ideally one would want the boy Pythagoras between the sticks. That night England had to make do with David Seaman, and the only equation he applied was: tragedy + distance = comedy. The yawning gap between the phalanx of defenders and the goalkeeper was so ludicrously vast it was bloody hilarious. Koeman could have comfortably curled a double-decker bus into the net without touching a soul. Sniggering with disbelief he jogged a few paces forward and scooped the ball delicately into the unguarded goal, before accepting a mobbing from his delirious teammates.

Over on the touchline the mood was less festive as Taylor berated the linesman for the actions of his fellow official: "You see, at the end of the day, I get the sack. Will you say to the fella, the referee has got me the sack... Thank him ever so much for that, won't you?" The bitter pill drawing up his bile was, of course, Koeman – for it was he that had brought down Platt minutes earlier. In the eyes of the English players and fans the Dutch sweeper should have been sitting in the dressing room, not hoofing the ball into their goal. As for the manager, well, he did like it not.

When England faced the Dutch three years later it was a very different story. Taylor was long gone – uprooted by a media campaign that somewhat surreally likened him to a turnip. (Route one – guilty as charged, but root vegetable?). His successor, Terry Venables, brought a certain style into the dugout and on to the pitch. The antidote to Taylor's bespectacled, tracksuited fidget, Venables evoked the sheepskin coat-wearing, Jag-driving style of management born in the 1970s. All roguish grins and shifty shoulders, Tel was hard to resist; my Irish grandmother, God rest her soul, was smitten: "Dat Terry Venables – sure, he's just a London spiv," she would comment approvingly whenever his grinning mug filled the screen.

The manager's swagger seeped slowly into the team until, one balmy June evening in 1996 at Wembley Stadium it erupted, quite unexpectedly, as a torrent of 'shexshee' football washed away the men in orange. Suddenly goals were flying in from all directions – the best, featuring a pair of lazy lay-offs followed by a rasping Alan

Shearer strike, brought to mind the Brazilians of 1970. It was the kind of display that English football fans had been dreaming about for years. A week later they awoke, bathed in the clammy sweat of a recurring nightmare – penalties, tears, Deutschland über alles.

As England prepared to embark on their 2010 World Cup odyssey against the US the weight of history hung heavily over the camp. The main focus of attention was on June 1950 and an infamous reversal against the same opponents. Resting Stanley Matthews from a stellar line-up including Wilf Mannion, Stan Mortensen and Tom Finney, England's 0-1 defeat to a scratch side of part-timers was so implausible that the initial wires home, assuming a misprint, relayed news of a 10-0 drubbing of the Yanks. Even the Americans were downbeat before the game; their coach William Jeffrey's rousing call to arms – 'we have no chance' – fell some way short of Act 3, Scene 1.

Spin forward several decades to June 1992 and we have another manager airing his thoughts ahead of a major tournament: "I expect to win it. Sit back, put your feet up in front of the TV, relax and enjoy it…" Having published Graham Taylor's hearty words on the eve of Euro '92, the tabloids gleefully heeled them back down his throat when England bombed out of the tournament after a series of pungent performances. The bitterness of the closing scenes stoked up the red tops' fury. Firstly, there was the substitution of goal-poaching national treasure Gary Lineker when all England needed was a goal, ideally one scored by a national treasure. Then we had the unedifying spectacle of cute-as-apple-pie Sweden striker Tomas Brolin – a man memorably described by David Baddiel as resembling a "very pretty pig" – ambling through the heart of the English defence to chip the ball past a stranded Chris Woods.

If we wind the clock forward a further year, to June 1993, we find England in the unlikely setting of the Foxboro Stadium in Boston, duking it out with Uncle Sam, in the hope of lifting a shimmering lump of off-season tinsel known as the 'US Cup'. You might argue that the moment when computer salesman Davide Gualtieri latched on to Stuart Pearce's deft through ball and beat David Seaman 8.3 seconds into England's game against San Marino represents the nadir of the Taylor stewardship. Maybe so, but the defeat in Boston provides the unstable fulcrum for England's 1990s adventures, teetering between the despair of Rotterdam in 1993, and delight in the rematch at Wembley in 1996. It was in Boston, chastened by the horror show of Euro '92, that English football acquired another mantra: No easy games at this level.

"There are no easy games at this level," Steven Gerrard revealed to the press gallery in Rustenburg a few days ahead of the opening match. Judging by his side's laboured, sweaty showing against local team Platinum Stars in their final warm-up game, the level in question may well have been 1,100m above the sea. But if Gerrard did harbour any doubts, they were not apparent as he strode into the Royal Bafokeng Stadium the following Saturday evening. He looked, as he always does, a model of focussed professionalism. This same look is evident when he faces the media, patiently regurgitating sound bites by rote – "yeah, no, obviously…" – but rarely revealing much in the way of a personality. He is, in fact, pretty much what one would expect to find at the helm of the Good Ship England as it sails into a World Cup campaign in the year 2010.

The word 'iconic' is grossly overused these days, usually by marketing gurus with eye-catching glasses and outré hairdos earnestly assuring us that: "Toilet Duck is such an *iconic* brand." Is Stevie Gerrard a modern, English footballing icon? To achieve iconic status the *Oxford English Dictionary* requires a person to be "regarded as representative of a culture or movement". Now then, after the 2006 World Cup the general consensus seemed to be that England's stand-out player was Owen Hargreaves, an energetic midfield technician with an unassuming, quietly professional aura; before 2010 many saw Gareth Barry, another midfield lynchpin, as the key figure. Do Hargreaves and Barry represent the culture of

England's football during the noughties? If so, Gerrard certainly fits the iconic bill. More romantically, 'iconic' may be defined as the depiction of "a victorious athlete in a conventional style". Twenty years ago when England returned from Italy, the figurehead at the front of the bus was Gazza, throwing off the despair of Turin by throwing a pair of bumptious comedy breasts over his England shell suit. A grinning, gurning figure of fun, sublime on the pitch, dafter than a brush off it – a *fin de siècle* English football icon, in the (then) conventional style.

Looking around the pitch at the Royal Bafokeng Stadium I struggled to spot anything remotely similar, until my eye alighted on Wayne Rooney, and the ghost of Gazza drifted across the shot. The darting eyes, the thick-set frame, the barely controlled excitement: the triumph of a love for playing the game over the fear of failure. Rolling the ball back and forth on his studs, hands on hips, surveying the scene, in his old-style England strip Rooney looked like a hero of times long past. A man, in short, crying out for some *izibongo*, the poetic praising used by local football fans to celebrate their favourite players.

There was once a fine crop of hand-picked monikers for English players, but the tradition seems to have been lost in the passing seasons. You have to go back to the seventies for the likes of Emlyn 'Crazy Horse' Hughes, Norman 'Bite Yer Legs' Hunter and Tommy 'the Anfield Iron' Smith, and further still to find the more evocative Stanley 'the Wizard of the Dribble' Matthews, John 'the Gentle Giant' Charles and Johnny 'the Maestro' Haynes. Perhaps these days the meticulous construction of brand identities around key players leaves little room for creative deviation. Take the two leading English centre forwards of the last fifteen years: Alan Shearer and Wayne Rooney. Their signature chants are hardly the product of rampant innovation – first up we have, 'Sheee-raaa!' and then – go on, have a wild guess, 'Rooo-neee!'.

Things are a bit different in South Africa where the fans wrap their favourites in complex mythologies through the use of *izibongo*, following the tradition of lionising warriors according to their exploits on the battlefield. The descriptive, personalised nature of these titles bestows a certain romance on the rudiments of running, kicking and tackling. How about Peter Sitsila, whose mastery of a moving ball earned him the title 'Jikeletshobeni' – he who controls the reins. Or Andries 'Pelepele' (hot like peppers) Mkwanazi. Fancy lining up against Jimmy 'Hitler' Shobi? – a notoriously robust midfield general from the great Pirates side of the 1930s, who, one assumes, had a tendency to drift out towards the right wing. The list is as endless as it is intriguing: Amos 'Heel Extension' Mkhari, Thomas 'Who's Fooling Who' Hlongwane, Harold 'Jazzy Queen' Legodi, Nkosi 'Let Them Dance' Molala, Lawrence 'Sister Monica' Siyangaphi, Lesley 'Slow Poison' Manyathela.

The English game seems a bit grey by comparison. The crowd might chant: "There's only one David Beckham," but it's not true – open the phone book, there are dozens. But a fiver says there really is *only* one Thabo 'Shaky-shaky' Mooki.

In South Africa such praise names provide a direct link between players and their fans in more ways than one. In fact certain names can actually influence the way that an individual performs. The prefix 'Ace', for example – most notably conferred on the great Chiefs player Ace Ntsoelengoe – carries with it a burden of style that must be carried onto the pitch. When he is in possession of the ball a bellow of 'Ace!' from the crowd instigates a change in tempo – the player bows his head, his shoulders slump and play slows to a walking pace. The crowd responds with another 'Ace!', this time, more sonorous and reverential, trailing out the sibilant into a prolonged hiss. Now the Ace protects the ball from opposing players, turning his back, dismissing their challenges with a shrug of his shoulders. As each is repelled the crowd responds with an 'Ace!', the pitch and excitement in the cry rising by degrees with each successive twist and turn. Eventually having asserted his dominance the Ace rolls the ball laconically to a teammate, at which point the crowd signs off with a final, ecstatic sigh of 'Aaaaaaaaaa-ce-ssssss!'.

The nearest equivalent to this I have seen in European football culture is the punctuation of a long, unbroken sequence of passing with shouts of 'olé!' but here the crowd participation is spontaneous and reactive. The beauty of the Ace ritual is that it is initiated and driven by the fans; they effectively control the actions of their player out on the pitch. This may only represent a symbolic connection, but it carries a significance that goes to the heart of the relationship between the South African football fan and the game.

Of course it can work both ways. Orlando Pirates' press officer Mickey Modisane swiftly earned the middle name 'Mouse', after using the PA system to bellow a cheerful welcome to two honoured Uefa delegates ahead of a Soweto derby: let's hear it for Michael Platini and Frank Beckenbauer.

The complaint that there are no longer any characters in the game is a well-worn mantra of English football punditry, but like many clichés it is founded to a large degree on fact. The likes of George Best in the 1960s and 70s, and Paul Gascoigne in the 1980s and 90s were colourful, instantly recognisable figures, who commanded the attention of the terraces with their skill and individual brilliance. As the Premier League has evolved and developed, the priorities for clubs, their playing staff and supporters have inevitably changed. Fans still pay an entrance fee and fork out for replica shirts, but the serious cash is provided by broadcast deals and sponsorship. Each league position in the Premiership is worth a hefty slice of Rupert's Sky money; the teams placed fifth and sixth can expect a windfall from Uefa. For the top four the cash cow that is the Champions League is waiting to be milked. Every match has its price; the difference between success and failure is measured in millions. What's a club to do? Invest in mercurial players to beguile opponents with their skill, and conjure up breathtaking goals in the style of Brazil's class of 1970? Rarely. Inter Milan's defeat of

Barcelona en route to the 2010 Champions League suggests a European ethic that promotes reality over fantasy – a rock-solid goalkeeper, impregnable defence, busy artisans staffing the midfield and a couple of lightning-fast alchemists to turn defence into attack at the drop of a hat.

At the start of the World Cup the most valuable player on the planet was Real Madrid's Portuguese winger Cristiano Ronaldo. A few years back, during his early seasons at Old Trafford, he was derided as a show pony for his excessive trickery. His party piece, a mesmeric series of steps over the rolling ball, was dismissed as fancy-dan histrionics, whereas in Brazilian football it is celebrated as the dance of the *pedaladas*. Funnily enough, once Cristiano started banging in the goals that powered United to the Premiership and Champions League titles, all was forgiven.

These days there is precious little room in the 'developed' world of football for extravagant skill just for the hell of it. Consequently, there is little call for praise names to connect the fans to the charming idiosyncrasies of talented players trying their luck. In fact the gulf between the fans and the millionaires they cheer on to the pitch has never been wider. If they do have a common bond it is an ever-sharpening focus on results, targets and end product. For a pastime that fills evenings and weekends and is supposed to provide a spot of diversion, possibly even escapism, that all sounds a bit too much like work, don't you think?

So, a praise name for Wayne. 'Wazza' sounds too derivative and as for 'Roo', all that conjures up is the image of an adorable infant marsupial beaming up at me from its mother's pouch. The young beast that springs to mind watching Rooney in full flow is far less cute. How about *Inkabi* – the bullock?

ROONEY AND HIS COLLEAGUES PITCHED THEIR CAMP IN Rustenburg, a rural backwater north of the bright lights of Jo'burg.

A quick glance at the 'town of rest' tells you that there is little on offer to entertain the full entourage. Things were very different in 2006 – the chic spa town of Baden-Baden never stood a chance once the WAGs moved in. With a collective trill of, 'Shoppin'!' they swept through its arcades and boutiques like a biblical plague. Stationed up in the Highveld, the players faced their own environmental crisis – the challenge of performing at dizzy heights. There were whispers that the England medical team might issue the players with Viagra to combat the effects of altitude sickness. Is a gaggle of bored WAGs and mandatory doses of Viagra a recipe for sporting success? Would we be adding 'post-coital fatigue' to the growing list of excuses for bombing out of a World Cup finals early doors? Questions that no doubt occurred to Fabio Capello shortly before he issued an edict banning WAGs from the camp.

Given the opulent surroundings most World Cup squads enjoy, the word 'camp' seems rather understated. Before the tournament began I headed across Jo'burg to Naturena, the HQ of the Kaizer Chiefs, hoping to watch the players train ahead of a key domestic fixture. All was still when I arrived. The security guard explained that the squad had gathered on the outskirts of town.

"Doing what?" I asked.

"Camping."

Indulge me for a moment. Using the present continuous tense conjugate the first five verbs you would normally associate with a group of modern, professional footballers passing a pleasant evening together. Do we have many 'campings'? Just as I was forming a mental image of John Terry and Frank Lampard in mud-spattered cagoules, giggling eagerly over a rusting billycan housing a swamp of tepid baked beans, the security guard enlightened me. Far removed from the British archetypes – wonky guy-ropes, sodden clothing, gingangoolies, the twanging Windsor bra strap, the flaring Williams nostrils – the South African version of camping, at least in the context of football, offers deeper cultural insights. In the late

19th and early 20th centuries, as pockets of organised football began to develop around the country, the practice of 'camping' echoed the ancient rituals that had once served as a precursor to battle. Players would remove themselves from the distractions of their home environment, and gather in a remote place to focus on the task ahead. In many cases they would be joined by a *sangoma*, the traditional healer, who would administer *muthi* – natural remedies – to bolster the courage and athletic prowess of the young men, and lessen that of their opponents.

These days, as the domestic game increasingly looks to Europe for its template, such rituals seem to be laughed off as the relic of a distant past. I once saw a rather smug English TV documentary on SABC that followed the earnest travails of the coach of a rural football club as he tried to arrest his team's poor run of form using the skills of the local *sangoma*. As each item was produced solemnly in the dressing room before the game – rat fat to make the wingers slippery fast, giraffe oil to strengthen the legs of the defenders, a monkey's paw to give the goalkeeper 'the grip that would never release' – the deadpan mockery of the narration stoked up the pathos, and with it my irritation. After all, the 'developed' world of sport is hardly immune from such indulgences, where players and fans adopt far less romantic methods to preserve their team's well-being: the insistence on the same seat in the stand, right sock on before left, loyalty to the same pair of fetid underpants for as long as the team keeps winning. It struck me that 'camping', with or without its *muthi* elements, is in essence a simple exercise in togetherness, designed to unite the group in readiness for the coming challenges. There are worse ways of doing this, as anyone who has attended a corporate bonding away-day that seamlessly combined readings from Sun Tzu's *The Art of War* with an afternoon of rowdy paintball will attest.

The England base in Rustenburg was their 'camp' but some of the more excitable elements in the press preferred 'gilded cage'. A place where the players could prepare in luxury, safe from the myriad dangers lurking beyond the razor-wire fence. Inevitably, questions over security dogged the global marketing of the 2010 World Cup. The fact that only 39 incidents of crime were reported during the 2009 Confederations Cup – a tournament that hosted almost 600,000 supporters – suggested that the South African security forces were on top of their game. Despite this, when the news broke that several Egyptian players had been robbed in their Johannesburg hotel, the doom-mongers perked up.

Six months later fingers were twitching back over the panic button. On January 8, on the road from Brazzaville to Cabinda, a chilling episode blighted the start of the 2010 African Nations Cup when the bus carrying the Togo national team was stranded in a hail of bullets. The driver and two Togolese team officials died. Elements of the media drew spurious connections between the murders in Angola and the perils awaiting visitors later that year at another African football tournament. But dust away the mud to examine the root causes of the ambush in Cabinda and you won't find problems peculiar to Africa. The factors underlying the gruesome attack are as globalised as the World Cup itself – occupation of a disputed territory, aftershocks of civil war, militant separatists, rivers of oil.

That is not to say that the host nation of the 2010 World Cup does not have a serious crime problem, because it clearly does. Crime statistics are notoriously malleable but whichever way you read them the numbers support the stereotypical view of South Africa as a dangerous place to be. Comparisons based on statistics compiled by international agencies such as the UN elevate the Republic to the top of the league tables for murder, assault and rape, the last of these registering a greater than 1 in 1000 incidence rate. Figures from the South African Police Service place annual reported murders around the 18,500 mark. For the UK the figure is close to 750. Of course, the ready availability of firearms separates this comparison but even compared with the States, the per capita rates place South Africa in a different league. In the lead up to 2010 much was made of the R130m (about £11.3m) funding for extra security and the intelligence-gathering programmes undertaken with specialist crime units around the globe. This seems like a sticking plaster rather than the cure to a disease with cells rooted deep within South African society.

Although I have been visiting South Africa for over a decade, the overbearing home security systems – invisible to those living with them – still catch my eye. In town pretty much every house has bars over the windows and doors and many driveways hide behind sliding iron gates. Each neighbourhood is hooked up to the local private security firm. These are not fripperies reserved for the rich and paranoid, just a basic necessity of everyday life. The only indicator of wealth is the level of service you subscribe to; a white-collar neighbourhood can call up a SWAT team, a mile away the blue-collar streets rely on the cycle patrol. I have listened to friends and relatives talk casually about minor burglaries, swiped mobile phones and car-jacks and occasionally allude to more scarring incidents that have befallen their own friends or colleagues. The prevailing view seems to be that crime is unacceptable, but accepted.

During lunch one day at my brother-in-law's farm near Plettenberg Bay he referred in passing to the theft of some kitchen goods – kettle, toaster, portable stereo – from a granny flat situated on the edge of his plot. He had driven into the nearby township and found some guys offering the items for sale. They handed everything back and that was that.

The natural beauties around his farm – sparkling dams and lagoons, dense pine forests, hills falling to lush rolling pastures, endless sandy beaches, handsome craggy mountains – cry out to me as the father of a young family fantasising about a wholesome lifestyle. The same call has drawn wealth to the area in the form of exclusive hotels, boutique shopping malls and gated riverside complexes. About a mile down the road from the farm is a polo club. With a helipad. On the fringes of these burgeoning new communities the wood, corrugated iron and unpainted breezeblocks of the townships sprawl. To state the blindingly obvious, any society with an unequal distribution of wealth is susceptible to crime and in South Africa the inequality of wealth distribution is blindingly obvious.

Closer to the start of the tournament, closer to England's base camp, the murder of Eugène Terre'Blanche raised the security question yet again. My initial exposure to Terre'Blanche was through the Nick Broomfield documentary *The Leader, His Driver and the Driver's Wife*. This angry, barking bear of a man with his icy, electric blue eyes, carefully manicured beard and pseudo-militaristic khaki fatigues seemed to represent the very worst of the exported stereotypes, immortalised in the *Spitting Image* song, *I've never met a nice South African*. Terre'Blanche was a standard bearer for the far right, establishing and leading the white supremacist movement Afrikaner Weerstandsbeweging, the AWB, a group that led white dissent during the volatile period before and after the release of Mandela.

Looking back now at footage of Terre'Blanche in his tub-thumping heyday, I cannot help thinking of Roderick Spode, the brilliant Oswald Mosley pastiche that Wodehouse slipped into the Jeeves and Wooster stories – a barnstorming orator harbouring the darkly destructive secret that he owned a boutique in Bond Street selling ladies' scants. Despite a spell in jail and a second equally damning Broomfield documentary – *His Big White Self* – Terre'Blanche and the AWB never completely went away. Internal problems within the ANC, rising crime and the ESKOM energy crisis all added to a general feeling of unrest and, more specifically, fuel for the lobby arguing that things were better in the 'good old days'. When, a matter of weeks before the tournament, Terre'Blanche was murdered by two farm workers in a dispute over pay, the local panic attacks sent shivers around the globe. "World Cup fans face bloodbath" hollered the *Daily Star*.

If these stories cast a few clouds over the English touring parties heading out to the Republic, it was nothing compared to the gunmetal blanket of grey they were leaving behind. 'England expects' is a well worn cliché, but this time it felt like the players shouldered a heavier burden than usual. Ahead of every major football tournament there is always hope and expectation, bubbling up around the country, coming to the boil as the kick-off date approaches. In the days and weeks leading up to the US game, the sheer volume of England flags that appeared – billowing from window sills, flapping on the sides of vans and cars – suggested deeper national emotions were stirring. Hope and expectation, of course – but what about *need*? After an endless, leaden winter and an unpleasantly bracing spring, the country seemed to be yearning for the warmth and levity of a long sporting summer.

On the day that England took on Platinum Stars in the final warm-up fixture the news from home was bleak. David Cameron warned of "difficult decisions", promising spending cuts to change our whole way of life. The prime minister was busy endorsing the tough measures that had helped Canada out of their fiscal hole in the mid-nineties. We cut from Cameron, frowning apologetically at the camera, to library pictures of a crowd gathered on a hill above Calgary, heard the boom of dynamite and then a few half-hearted whoops as, down in the city bowl, an unsustainable general hospital crumbled into dust. I guess that's the kind of policy you gloss over in your manifesto: 'If elected we will start blowing up hospitals' would surely never get past the spin doctors. And then there was Derrick Bird, an unassuming, well-liked local man who left home one spring morning to embark on a journey along the picturesque Cumbrian coast, leaving a trail of broken bodies and lives behind him.

All things considered, I think it's fair to say that on June 12 2010, the English people were ready for a spot of escapism – a couple of weeks, hopefully more, in which they could abandon themselves to a whole new set of anxieties. To borrow from the bulging lexicon of football cliché, what the nation needed was an arm round the shoulder, not another kick up the backside.

And what did they get? A game in which England were damned by voices from the past and wizardry from the future. First we had Fabio Capello, departing from the script in his final press conference by inadvertently spitting out a mouthful from an earlier vintage – Taylor '92: "I expect to win it." Whatever happened to no easy games at this level? And then there was the looming, unwelcome shadow of progress.

A football's a football, right? Wrong. Just ask Fifa, Uefa and their chums at Adidas. Prior to each international tournament there is an ungainly scramble to redesign, redevelop and re-brand the faithful old bladder. Remember the Roteiro at Euro 2004? A silver sphere scarred with black daggers, it looked like an unconvincing prop from a late-eighties sci-fi porn film. World Cup 2010 was no exception. Ahead of the tournament much was made of the ground-breaking techniques used to create "an energetic unit" that was "perfectly spherical". A round ball. Who knew?

He/she/it was called *Jabulani*, Zulu for 'hey, let's celebrate!' The goalkeepers weren't joining in. England legend Gordon Banks voiced concerns prior to the game, saying: "I used to pride myself on my positioning, but if you work hard to get that right and then the ball moves all over the place when you think you've got a chance of holding on to it, then it's destroying the art." David James's pre-match verdict was an unhappy marriage of honesty and pragmatism: "…the ball is dreadful. It's horrible, but it's horrible for everyone."

James was watching from the safety of the bench when things got really horrible. Shortly before the end of a half in which England had looked relatively assured, Fulham's Clint Dempsey hoofed a speculative shot at the England goal. The ball skipped off the turf, kissed Robert Green's gloves and then twirled away from the despairing keeper to dribble over the line. The first weekend of the World Cup was not so much rollercoaster as ghost train: first the screamer, now the howler.

Before a big match, as their head sinks into the pillow, I assume all elite sports folk allow their subconscious to dream up the ideal scenario: a wonder goal, the winning runs, chipping in from the bunker. But surely, left to its own devices, the sporting brain must also sometimes drift into darker corners: the red card, the golden duck, the missed three-footer. Green's calamitous, bar o' soap moment was, to borrow from Gore Vidal, via Kevin Keegan, "a perfect nightmare".

As part of their pre-tournament acclimatisation, Capello had taken his men to Austria to try out the new ball at altitude. Green's delicate post-match comments – "It may well have moved. I don't often miss a ball like that ... not by that much ..." – elicited a swift, curt retort from across the border in Herzogenaurach. The view from the Adidas HQ was unequivocal. "We believe it was down to a massive goalkeeping mistake and Green should examine his own achievements as the ball came towards him." He didn't get the chance. The following week, when the first Algerian shot headed towards the England goal it was James, not Green, watching his life flash before him. The Sunday papers also voiced opinions: "Hand of Clod", led the *Mirror*. Dodgy ball or dodgy keeper? Either way we were back in familiar England territory: perceived injustice, palpable ineptitude.

If technology was at fault for the goal England conceded it also had a hand in the one they scored. Viewers of ITV's HD coverage were whisked away to view an affordable family hatchback shortly before Emile Heskey set up his skipper's goal. For those households – listening in baffled horror to their neighbours' joyful hooting – it was a Zen goal, existing only in the perception of those with cheaper tellies.

An early goal for a German or Italian side would be a down payment guaranteeing a safe return, but this was England; at 1-0 seasoned followers eased forward onto the edges of their seats and stayed there. Any highlights package of England's recent adventures in major tournaments will inevitably focus on the tenacious comebacks, stirring rearguards and agonising near-misses. Setting aside the glorious aberration of the Dutch at Wembley in 1996, recent history tells us that the idea of England using an early goal as a platform upon which to construct an adroit, comfortable victory is faintly ludicrous. And so it proved in the Royal Bafokeng Stadium. From the high point of the fourth minute, England tumbled into a spot of half-time slapstick, before staggering towards the final whistle. Rooney was quiet; Heskey spoiled an evening of honest toil by punting a golden opportunity into the keeper's breadbasket. In truth, England's best forward on the night was probably the right-back Glen Johnson, cranking up the vuvuzelas with a series of darting runs sprinkled with deft tsamayas.

After the game the players and management were swift to accentuate the positives: a point in the bag; two more games to come; not a bad result against decent opposition. There really are no easy games at this level. The following evening Germany wiped the floor with the Socceroos.

How did *they* cope with the new match ball? I guess their biggest complaint was that they were sick of the sight of the Jabulani, seeing as they'd been using it in the Bundesliga since before Christmas. Nicht vorbereitet, vorbereitet zu scheitern, as they say. The German performance was a class apart from anything else in the first week; the young Turk Mesut Özil scribbling his name on to the post-tournament shopping lists of the plutocrats of European football. Equally exciting were the other surnames on their team sheet: Boateng, Aogo, Cacau, Gomez. An inevitable theme of a South African World Cup was the power of sport as a unifying force. Some were sniffy about Germany's cosmopolitan squad, but stepping back to view the bigger picture surely there are reasons to be cheerful here.

And England? With almost a week to fill before the Algerians in Cape Town the players could settle down to some long-range shooting practice. As for the popular press, there were no hoolies in the town or drunken revels in the camp to fulminate over, but in Green there was a scapegoat to roast on the braai – death by a thousand puns – and an 'I told you so' or two for Capello to chew over: Heskey can't finish, Ledley won't last.

All a tad gloomy. What the camp needed was some inspiration. Where better to look than to the great man, Madiba: "The greatest glory in living lies not in never falling, but in rising every time we fall." And if that was too wordy there was always Iain Dowie's pithier version to fall back on: at this level it's all about "bouncebackability".

NELLY THE ELOQUENT

A FEW WEEKS BEFORE THE START OF THE WORLD CUP I WAS sitting in the coffee shop of a large antiquated bookshop on Charing Cross Road, wallowing in nostalgia. I had just bought a copy of *One Night in Turin* – Pete Davies's superb account of Italia '90 – and was flicking through the photos: Toto Schillaci caught between joy and disbelief as his hot scoring streak rolled on, red cards for Rijkaard and Völler – a double bubble perm dismissal – Cameroon's ecstatic bundle as they led England, Gazza and Butcher saluting the crowd, Diego and co. berating the referee. An evocative snapshot of an unforgettable few weeks.

I had first read the book during the summer of 1998 in its original incarnation as *All Played Out*, in the very same room, then in *its* original incarnation as the bookshop's maths and science department. Back then, reliving Paul Gascoigne's emergence onto the international stage had a certain poignancy, as he had just been elbowed off it when Glenn Hoddle made his final squad cut for the World Cup in France. I was working in the bookshop that summer, splitting my time between reading about the heroic failure of 1990 and trying to ignore the murderous glare of Greta.

Greta was, and possibly still is, a tiny, wizened, desperately embittered Swede. She had run the maths and science department for many decades and was clearly livid about it. For Greta the question was not: is my glass half-full or half-empty? It was: hey, who stole my glass and replaced it with a turd? And why is this turd cold? And why do I only get one? And so on. Every morning she would shuffle in, jabbing a bony finger at the Heavens, shaking her head in disgust.

"Oh my gaad, dis vedder. I sink now dat dis is too much."

It was too hot, too cold, too wet, too dry, too windy, too calm. Whatever it was, the "vedder" was always too much. She would then cast an icy glare around the department, until her gimlet eye alighted on a book spine jutting a few millimetres proud of its peers on the shelf. She would look at me, smile sadly, and shake her head.

"Vell den. Oh my gaad, dis place. I am sinking dat maybe it is turning into some kind of a pig style."

I would study the faded carpet in sheepish acknowledgement of the fact that, once again, I had failed to deliver the precise level of order she required: a style I would come to know as OCD by Ikea. For the vast majority of the day our room was deserted, and I busied myself by reading, dusting the shelves under her steely gaze and wondering how I had come to star in my very own Ingmar Bergman tragedy. The mood only broke at one o'clock when she headed out for lunch. Within five minutes of her departure the room was full, flooded with teachers and professors from every maths department and faculty in London grabbing armfuls of books on calculus, Game Theory, fractals and superstrings. For the next 50 minutes, I was besieged. Fermat's Last Theorem? It was more like Custer's Last Stand. At five to two they fled; at two she returned.

To make matters worse the shop operated a sales commission system to augment the piffling wages. While Greta was there the cash register was an ornament gathering dust; during the brief retail frenzy that I oversaw every lunchtime it would pour with smoke and occasionally catch fire. Though she never understood its rationale, this imbalance in our fortunes chipped away at an already brittle relationship. The glue that bonded us was Fatty the pigeon, a filthily grey ball of exhaust-smoked feathers that waddled around on the windowsill safe in the knowledge that once a day Greta would come and tip a loaf of breadcrumbs into its gaping, pink maw. Thus fortified he would corner an unsuspecting female and, following an ugly scuffle, haul his bloated carcass aboard for a brief, deeply unpleasant coupling. On the other side of the glass his patron, arms folded, watched this tawdry scene play out with grim satisfaction. She would then turn to me and say: "Oh my gaad, I sink dat Fatty is up to dese tricks again."

And then she would smile, the scowling mask cracked, the room lit up. I would look over, nod and grin and the mood in the maths and science department lifted a few inches. Soon enough Fatty would fall sideways off his struggling mount, sated, and the spell would break. Greta would spot a title on chaos theory an inch out of place and let slip a thunderous tut, and I would return to my dusting.

Inevitably in life it is the extreme characters that stay with us, signposts in our long-term memory back to a period in the past. For me Greta will always represent the negative, inflexible, no-can-do, traits of human behaviour. Happily, in a small town in the north of Limpopo, I stumbled across her opposite number – Nelly.

The journey began back in 2008 shortly after the unveiling of the official World Cup 2010 mascot. We were staying with friends in Johannesburg and I spotted a piece in the paper about Zakumi – a jolly-looking cartoon leopard with a mop of green hair. There were quotes from administrators and former Bafana players welcoming this cheerful addition at a time when the tournament preparations were somewhat fraught. But as I read on a spokesman for either SAFA or Fifa took things further, and suddenly we were into paradigm shifts and dynamic branding. As I read more, my blood started to boil – an iconic emblem ideal for building stakeholder partnerships? Surely it's a lovely, big pretend leopard? – until my eyes alighted on a picture further down the page. Suddenly I had left the grey world of corporate branding and could see sunshine, smiles and hope. Suddenly I could see Nelly. A small picture accompanying a brief report from a local newspaper about a woman running a football team in a minor league in a small town. It wasn't much, but it was enough. An hour of Googling and a few phone calls later yielded a mobile phone number. Now I just had to get there.

Early on a Tuesday morning I headed out of the city by a circuitous route. Unlike London where the daily trudge into work spreads the pain across trains, buses, tubes and cars, in Johannesburg – as in most South African cities – the roads are the favoured option and the rush hour traffic is spectacular. Like a middle-aged dad sinking into an old sofa in front of *The Guns of Navarone* after a weighty Sunday roast, Johannesburg spreads and sprawls in a relaxed, careless sort of way. Not so much a defined city as a collision of different places – Sandton, Benoni, Soweto, Kempton Park, Germiston – each with their own structure and identity. In town planning terms it puts me in mind of a jigsaw bent and twisted together by a determined toddler. The rolls and undulations do at least give one a sense of place and perspective – if London had Johannesburg's curves you could stand on the doorstep of the Hackney Empire and gaze up across town at its sister in Shepherds Bush.

Eventually I had escaped the outer reaches of the city and was flying up an arrow-straight highway heading north. The strip of tar stretching far into the distance – shimmering and molten under the sun's glare – was a constant, but the landscape it carried me through revealed subtle variations. Mile upon mile of mealie fields gave way to rough grazing land where cattle clustered around the shade and meagre bounty of a few spindly acacia trees; next a forest of towering sunflowers, which in turn rolled into soft grasslands supporting bulbous, sand-coloured anthills several feet high. With the sun reaching its height I sped past places at one with their unforgiving surroundings – Bela Bela (boiling, boiling), Warmbad (warm bath) – and soon enough had arrived in Polokwane.

It was here in this small, rural town that the opening lines of the second chapter in the history of post-Apartheid South Africa were written. Despite being one of the architects of the new order, former president Thabo Mbeki never quite managed to outrun the shadow of his charismatic predecessor. While Mandela was a morally courageous leader and inspiring orator, the perception of Mbeki was of an academic, slightly aloof figure, ill-equipped or simply unwilling to grasp and shake the twin pillars of South African moral panic: AIDS and Zimbabwe. In Polokwane in December 2007 the ANC Conference ushered in a new leader, effectively a president-elect, promising a fresh approach to problems at home and diplomacies abroad. The controversial Jacob Zuma swept into office, cheered home by a boisterous mob of supporters chanting his anthem *Lethu Mshini Wami* – bring me my machine gun.

Zuma's victory was short-lived. Ten days after the Conference he was indicted by the Scorpions – South Africa's organised crime unit – on corruption charges. The allegations concerned government arms deals and were foreshadowed by the 2005 conviction of Schabir Shaik, Zuma's financial adviser, on similar charges. The Shaik affair had led Mbeki to relieve Zuma of his role as ANC deputy president. Six months later his reputation suffered another thumping blow, following rape accusations made by the daughter of one of his late friends. Zuma was acquitted but the damage was done. During the trial it emerged that he had known that the young woman was HIV positive but had thought that a shower after unprotected sex would reduce his risk of contracting the virus. At the time he was the head of the National AIDS Council. Like any country where politics is ingrained in the fabric of everyday life, the South African media boasts a vibrant parody and satire community. Following Zuma's trial, they took him apart.

In September 2008 the High Court in Pietermaritzburg declared the Scorpions indictment unlawful, but Judge Nicholson's ruling went further, straying into more personal territory. He found it "unfortunate" that the indictment had come so soon after Mbeki's defeat in Polokwane. Refuting the judge's inference that he had meddled in the process, Mbeki resigned from the presidency and lodged an appeal with the Supreme Court in Bloemfontein. In

January 2009 they overturned the ruling on the procedure point and made clear that further comments suggesting political interference had been beyond the jurisdiction of the High Court.

In April 2009 the National Prosecuting Authority announced that it was dropping all charges against Zuma, leaving him clear to contest the general election later that month. Even after he had been sworn in as president the storm clouds refused to clear when the main opposition party, the Democratic Alliance, called for a judicial review of the NPA's timely decision.

It is still too early to say which man will leave the deeper footprints on South African political life, as they stumble along the trail blazed by Mandela's giant strides. All one can say with any certainty is that the pair are chalk and cheese. To clutch at a football metaphor, if Thabo Mbeki is the dependable centre-half, forever knocking the ball sideways to a nearby teammate, Jacob Zuma comes across as the tyro striker, shoulder charging defenders, berating the linesman and winking to the crowd between outrageous shibobos. In his younger days Zuma was, in fact, a famously robust centre-half, taking few prisoners during the lively matches played in the Robben Island League. But more of that later.

I had a particular reason for wanting to stop in Polokwane. To host matches in the World Cup group stages, they first needed to sling up a sparkly new stadium. After a mild bout of exploration I arrived at the Peter Mokaba Stadium. A former president of the South African Youth Congress, Mokaba was a key figure in the Struggle during the State of Emergency in the 1980s. Like Zuma, Mokaba also had an eye-catching slogan – "Kill the Boer, kill the farmer" – and later in his political career courted further controversy by lobbying against the use of anti-retroviral medication in the treatment of AIDS. Ironically, it has been speculated that the disease ended his life prematurely at the age of 43.

The stadium bearing his name was fairly typical of the sports venues that serve communities in South Africa outside of the big cities. A running track encircled a pitch, overlooked by a stand on one side, with grassy banks offering less formal seating running around the remainder of the perimeter. The stand was a handsome structure covered with dagger-shaped concrete moulds, packed across its façade like the scales of a fish. The floodlight towers sported barber-shop stripes and looked striking and cheerful as they rose from the lush grass banks into a deep blue sky. But the most arresting feature of the stadium was the activity taking place within it. Bear in mind that this was midday in mid-summer in one of the hottest regions of the country. In spite of this, around the running track and across the pitch, young children were flogging themselves to death: it was only school sports day, for pity's sake. I saw two false starts in the 100 metres when small girls leapt from their marks ahead of the gun, wriggling and blowing the fingers they had just singed on the track. I saw a young lad pick up a white hot javelin, release an agonised "eish!" and hurl it several miles into a neighbouring field.

I walked around the grass verge surrounding the track. To my left, about a quarter of a mile away, a copse of cranes marked the site of the new Peter Mokaba stadium. Peering through the perimeter fence I could see a hive of dusty activity – trucks, hardhats and shouting – in the middle of which a rectangular concrete seating block lay cornered by four cylindrical turrets. The overall shape put me vaguely in mind of the San Siro, the Milanese stadium renovated in a similarly tubular style for the 1990 World Cup. Gazing at the chaotic building site before me, I was acutely aware of the gulf separating a tournament like Italia '90 – a sporting feast laid on by a wealthy European state whose population gorge themselves on football – with the uncertainties hanging over the World Cup's long-awaited debut on the African continent.

The controversy surrounding the South African bid to host the event stretches back to the turn of the century. In July 2000, when Fifa delegates were called to decide upon the destination of the

2006 tournament, Charles Dempsey, a 78-year-old known in his native New Zealand as Steptoe (thanks to a passing likeness for the late, great Wilfred Bramble), abstained from the voting, defying the orders of the Oceania Football Conference. He would not elaborate on his motives – "I had very strong reasons, but I'm not going into them" – but the whiff of foul play hung heavy in the air. As it was, in 2006 Germany put on a show that ran like clockwork but lacked a compelling central narrative. That was until Zinedine Zidane dragged his ageing side to the brink before performing a final bow on the world stage in the form of a darting head-butt into the chest of an Italian defender.

One school of thought suggests that South Africa would not have been able to deliver the infrastructure upgrade in time for 2006. Even after the success of the 2010 bid, the whispering campaign hissed on. Instead of being a source of great anticipation and national pride the tournament became a problem for the ANC, a monkey on their back pulling their hair and flicking their ears. For every ESKOM fiasco, township crime wave, inflation spike or loss suffered by Bafana Bafana, the media hoisted the 'Where does this leave 2010?' banner to flutter and twitch above the heads of the administrators. In 2006 Christmas came early for the harbingers of doom when rumours began to circulate that Fifa were looking at fallback options in Asia, Europe, perhaps even Down Under.

As in Australia, the oval ball looms large in South African sporting life. It is an indicator of the cultural and social divisions that separate the football codes in the Republic that the existing rugby grounds played only a supporting role in 2010. Choosing a long, uphill route signposted by Fifa, the tournament organisers undertook to build several new stadiums from scratch, and spread the load far and wide.

Watching the country gearing up for such a huge event, one could almost hear the slow, collective intake of breath; the stakes were so high. In his national address in January, Jacob Zuma identified 2010 as the most important year for the country since 1994: "The year 2010 must be the year in which for the first time we all communicate positive messages about our country to the world – the successes and possibilities. We have to put the culture of negativity behind us."

A rugby pitch separates the new Peter Mokaba stadium from the old, and as I walked around its edge a school minibus pulled up and unloaded a gaggle of young children. They ran on to the grass whooping with excitement, chasing rugby balls and footballs – boys and girls, black and white, probably no more than seven or eight years old – and stopped me dead in my tracks. The sleight of hand passes, the dummies, the shibobos, the barefoot drop goals, the long rallies of head tennis; it was stunning. It dawned on me that sport is in the blood of South Africa; if it can wriggle free of the partiality and prejudices from its past, the world had better watch out.

I drove out of Polokwane and picked up the road to Tzaneen, following the highway through open farmlands, broken by the occasional cluster of thatched rondavels, miles from the nearest signs of human life. I passed a line of children walking to school along a dusty track bisecting a field of tall grass. They looked immaculate. Pressed grey shorts, stiff, brilliant white shirts, navy blue knee-length socks. Recently I've become slightly obsessed with school uniforms, and not in that way. As a parent stumbling inexorably towards a labyrinthine world of league tables, Ofsted reports and catchment areas, adherence to a school uniform suddenly seems important. When we used to live in Hackney the sight of a group of schoolkids put the fear of God into me: bandanas, jewellery, baseball caps, trainers, low-slung trousers showcasing designer briefs. A tiny voice in my head – admittedly one that belonged to a gruff, retired brigadier with wildly bushy eyebrows and a complexion like salami – would snort: "I can't believe you are going to school looking like *that*". I'm not suggesting that the youth of our inner cities should be bowling along, arms linked, sporting striped blazers and straw boaters, just that maybe school uniforms are somehow indicative of a level of respect for yourself and the education process. (Blimey, what have I become? Time to dash off a letter to *The Telegraph* on the subject, while champing furiously on the stem of my pipe). The point I am tortuously trying to make is that the happy little crocodile of kids I saw snaking their way through the fields in Limpopo that day had nothing, at least by Western standards, but their mothers would clearly be damned before sending them to school looking anything less than a million dollars.

I began to climb up from the valley floor, nosing into the hills on a narrowing, increasingly curvaceous road. On either side of the road, crumbling banks of terracotta earth created vantage points for sheep and goats to gaze impassively at passing cars. As I ascended further the eucalyptus trees gave way to towering pines which threw cooling shadows across the road and filled the air with a clean, fresh scent. I pulled over at a clearing fenced by a line of ramrod straight trees; all I could see between their slender trunks was blue sky and a few wisps of white cloud. It felt like the top of the world. Over the foot-high wall separating the road from certain death below, I could see the beautiful breadth of the Letaba River oozing between lush grazing pastures before describing a sharp dog-leg back towards a dark green blanket of forest. I phoned Nelly and made arrangements to meet in the Spur Restaurant.

Eventually I arrived in Tzaneen, a substantial rural settlement surrounded by fruit groves and plantations, nestling in the foothills of the Wolkberg Mountains. I entered the welcoming cool of the restaurant and looked around for Nelly. My only previous sight of her had been the grainy image from the newspaper. Only two tables were occupied, one by a 17st white farmer with a bushy ginger beard, the other by a smiling, middle-aged black woman waving eagerly in my direction. A slight figure immaculately dressed in a traditional wrap-around dress clipped at the shoulder, with her hair scraped back from her head showing off wide, hooped earrings, Nelly carried the unmistakable air of a quietly determined soul.

Nelly explained that she worked as a counsellor in a health clinic outside Tzaneen, steering young people away from drink and drugs and trying to educate them about the necessity for safe sex.

I asked a leading question.

"How did you end up running a football team?"

"I will never forget that day; it was a Tuesday. Driving home from work I saw a group of boys sitting around in the shade of a tree, having a dop [drink] and smoking dagga. When I asked them what they were doing they said that they were bored – they had just matriculated and now there was nothing to do. I asked them what they liked doing. They said soccer. The next day I bought a ball and when I drove past their spot, I threw it out of the window. 'Go, get on with it,' I told them. I saw them play and they were good – it got them off their backsides, running about, they looked happier. Then I saw the reports of the local league in the newspaper. I wanted them to be involved in something, to get away from the drink and dagga and trouble, and told the boys they should join up, but they said that even to register cost R1,000. They had collected R120 from gambling games; I said that I could not help with the rest, it was too much. I told them to go away and earn some more money. A week later they found me, they were full of pride: 'We've got more money.' 'How much?' I asked. 'R180.' I laughed, but now I had a problem. I wanted to help these boys, but I am not rich. I slept well and went to the bank the next morning.

"The boys were mad with excitement and ran to the league offices to register. When they came back they had special ID badges – now they were part of something important, it really meant a lot to them. They were laughing and asking if I would support them. I said that I would, of course I would. 'No, but really,' they said. 'I will, I will,' I told them. Then one of the boys showed me his card up close. The name of their team was *Nelly's All Stars* and they had registered *me* as their coach and manager. I was furious. 'What can I do? I don't know about soccer!' They just laughed and said it would be fine. Now we had another problem – they needed uniforms and these things cost big money. Luckily my brother runs a team – the Majamela Dangerous Darkies – and he let me have some of their old kit."

Nelly paused and fixed me with a keen, engaging look.

"Now we were ready to kick off. The evening before a match the boys would want to come to stay at my place, camping. We must be together, they said. So I'm cooking for them and they sleep wherever they can find space: by the door, on the stoep [verandah], on the garage roof. And when they played their matches, they were good: quick and tricky – full of cheeky nonsense – but scoring some nice goals. But now another problem comes along: corruption. These are small, local leagues – people know people – sometimes a manager from another team, perhaps he has a business in town and can offer something to a referee. This corruption, this is a big problem – it makes me sick and the boys get mad when they know that the game is not played fair. They want to klap [hit] the referee and now I can see them getting into problems with the police. I supported this team to get these boys out of trouble, not drop them into it.

"The last straw came on the prize-giving day for the season just passed. The boys knew that they had come second in the league, but they were called in fifth. They were crying and angry and kept asking me what had happened. So I took the decision to take my team out of the league. Now the administrators start crying. You know, it was a big deal having a woman in charge of a team, they liked it. But when I attended a meeting with them and looked them in the eye and said: 'Now what are you going to do about this corruption?' they rolled their eyes and shrugged and could not answer me. So I decided to do my own thing by setting up the Love Life Games. Every month we have a tournament – we keep it simple, different coloured T-shirts for each team, we play for a cup;

whoever won it last time, brings it back and defends it. The boys are happy again. This is why I got involved in the first place. It's simple, I believe that soccer should be a way of keeping fit, staying out of trouble, having fun and winning some pride; getting the chance to move on and up. I have written to Shakes and Jomo about my boys, telling them to send scouts. The boys tell me to look out for them on the big screen in 2010."

As I looked at Nelly, chattering away, brimming with cheerful optimism, I wondered how realistic these aspirations were – a wondrous shibobo in a field in Limpopo is a bit like the Zen tree falling in the woods – but that is not really the point. She had belief and hope and an iron will to do the best she could for her boys. She could talk for South Africa, and she was so positive, so certain, so eloquent that you had to believe every word.

While I felt inspired by Nelly's outlook, her tale of petty malpractice was depressingly familiar. Corruption in sport is no joke but try this one: how many referees does it take to blow a whistle? In South Africa the answer seems to be 20: one to blow, 19 to face corruption charges based on his evidence. This scenario began to unfold at the turn of the century when Moses Soko, a referee, admitted to accepting bribes from certain club owners. His confessions implicated many other officials and led to a formal SAFA investigation. They also earned him half a dozen bullets – he was ambushed and shot but survived. Four years later a formal police enquiry, under the Ealing Comedy codename Operation Dribble, resulted in over 40 arrests, amongst them a score of match officials. A year later the High Court ordered SAFA to reinstate the referees; three years after that, a number of them sued the Federation for lost earnings.

It is hard to say what ultimately became of Operation Dribble. It seems to have dribbled away quietly amid speculation that the scale of wrongdoing and profile of those likely to be implicated argued for a tactical withdrawal. Whether or not this is true, it is clear that the rumours and suspicions persist. During the 2009 Premier League season, SAFA's Referees Appointment Committee announced the extreme measure of introducing polygraph tests for officials in an attempt to weed out those with knowledge of sharp practices. Certain people within South Africa will pounce on such stories – see how 'they' run 'their sport' – echoing similar sentiments to those they express on hearing the latest scurrilous tales from within the ANC. We outsiders looking in can nod sagely – well, that's Africa for you: power corrupts – conveniently ignoring our own shortcomings: the moats, the duck ponds, the flipping houses.

I asked Nelly how her family had reacted to her involvement in football.

"At first they were unsure. I've got five daughters – maybe they wondered what was going on when all these boys were coming camping at our place. But I know that they understand why I do these things."

We left the restaurant and walked back to the car. Although the sun was now dipping fast, the heat was still oppressive. We drove out of Tzaneen through mango and papaya groves and turned off the main road in the direction of Nelly's village. The quality of the road surface grew steadily worse until we were sliding along on a stony dust track. We seemed to be heading for a popular destination. The track was lined with people making slow but steady progress: women walking sedately under the teetering bulk of washing balanced on their heads, men crouched over wheelbarrows full of firewood or shards of reclaimed metal, a few head of cattle being coaxed along with flimsy-looking sticks.

Eventually the road ended at a circular turning point, bordered by a few spindly acacia trees and a couple of shacks made of wood and corrugated iron. At the end of the working day the place was buzzing with movement and life. There was shouting, waving, laughing, a few children crying. Dogs roamed, chickens pecked and strutted. Rusting bakkies loaded with fruit putted in and out. An

ancient but rather handsome bus – white with green and red stripes
– sat on the farthest edge of the clearing, packed to the roof but
still welcoming latecomers, pointing towards a track that made the
one we had driven in on look like a velvet carpet. I said goodbye to
Nelly and watched her walk serenely into the crowd. The heat was
unrelenting, everything was in the wrong place – Greta would have
hated it – but somehow it all seemed to work. It was a colourful,
lively scene in which order battled with chaos armed only with a
communal sense of purpose.

Reading the article about the mascot had made me want to
punch myself in the temple. By contrast an hour spent with Nelly
was both calming and inspiring. A person of unimpeachable
integrity trying to do the right thing, to make things better for
those around her. As I walked back to the car, I appointed her my
unofficial mascot for the 2010 World Cup representing not an
iconic emblem for building stakeholder partnerships, but rather a
set of qualities: humility, tenacity, humanity, that would serve the
tournament far better.

Driving back down the gravel road I passed a group of shacks
clustered close to the side of the track. Fires were now burning as
the preparations for the evening meal got underway. A group of
young boys barefoot, in ragged shorts, were mobbed around a focal
point, kicking up a storm of thick, red dust. Speeding past I caught
a glimpse of what must once have been a football – now a ragged,
deflated carapace – amongst the flailing feet. Suddenly the former ball
leapt from the dust and looped between a pair of stakes supporting
a washing line. Goal. The scorer ran into the road bellowing, arms
raised above his head in frantic celebration, pursued by an angry
matriarch gesticulating at her laundry. Watching them disappearing
slowly in my wing mirror brought to mind the only intelligible piece
of knowledge I managed to extract from my long days spent dusting
books under Greta's steely gaze. It is a line from James Gleick's
Pulitzer Prize-nominated *Chaos: making a new science*:

"Our feeling for beauty is inspired by the harmonious arrangement of order and disorder..."

It struck me that if the 2010 World Cup – or, for that matter, African football – needs a slogan, it should look no further.

WHATEVER HAPPENED TO
THE DANGEROUS DARKIES?
(PART 1)

BRAZIL'S THIRD GOAL IN THE 1970 WORLD CUP FINAL IS WIDELY regarded as being one of the finest ever scored. The fun starts when Clodoaldo throws a series of lavishly outrageous samba swerves into a stroll across the midfield. On the face of it these gyrations were designed to wrong-foot opponents thereby creating space for teammates. On a more basic level, the underlying message they sent to the Italians was clear enough: "Gentlemen, I'm afraid we're just too good for you – look, we've even got time to dick about." The ball is then rolled nonchalantly out to Rivelino on the left wing who scoops it up the touchline to Jairzinho. The midfielder ghosts past his marker before slipping a pass between a pair of hapless defenders to the edge of the penalty area. Happily, the ball comes to rest at the feet of the greatest player in the history of the game, Edison Arantes do Nascimento.

The scenes that follow challenge Ali's rope-a-dope haymaker in Zaire for the title of the iconic sporting images of the last century. In slow motion Pelé effortlessly assumes control of the ball and then, as every non-Italian in the world screams linguistic variations on the theme of 'Go on! Take it on! Have a shot!' he side-foots the ball lazily to his right, to dribble a few yards away from goal. It's pathetic, it's useless, it's rubbish. It's bloody brilliant. Unnoticed by everyone on the planet except Pelé, Carlos Alberto is haring up the right wing. The pass is inch perfect; there's no need to even stop, he just elongates his stride through the ball, lashing it into the corner of the Azzurri's net. Goal. Goaaaaaaaaaal! Goaaaaaaaaaaaaaaaaaaaaaaaaaaaaaal!!!

For the generation watching that match, the perfect goal from the Beautiful Team raised a hopelessly unrealistic level of expectation of what could be achieved when a group of blokes punting a ball around a field really put their minds to it. But it is not just the sumptuous build-up play and rasping shot that makes that move, that match, that team, so special. The three World Cup finals prior to 1970 had produced their fair share of memorable moments – Brazilian brilliance in 1958 and again in 1962; to this day England fans are still gnawing at the bones of the feast laid on four years later. But these tournaments were relayed through the shadows and fog of black and white television. In 1970, in the burning glare of a Mexican summer, for the first time the World Cup exploded into glorious, gaudy colour. The goal that crowned the champions was the pot of gold at the end of this newly discovered rainbow.

For the world of sports broadcasting, colour represented a straightforward proposition – progress and change for the greater good. In other branches of televised entertainment colour raised deeper, more complex issues that were far harder to integrate seamlessly into mainstream culture. Take humour, for example. As a child watching situation comedies in the 1970s an underlying message, whispered in the clipped tones of a 1940s public information film, was often just audible beneath the jovial surface nonsense: "Beware! Foreigners and coloured people are different; as such they are both funny and potentially dangerous." You could see it in the wide-eyed terrors of Rigsby in *Rising Damp*, watching Miss Jones's nostrils flare with lust whenever the black lodger Philip – the 'son of a chief' (from Croydon) – entered stage left. As a family we all settled down to chortle at *Mind Your Language* – a comedy set in a language school that relied entirely on the *Beano*-style antics of its students. The show assembled a United Nations of hackneyed, racial stereotypes, complete with catchphrases that landed periodically with a reassuring thud. The wobbly-headed Indians were apologetic, "a thousand apologies, masterjee", the

Chinese students likewise, "velly, velly solly", the Spanish were confused "por favor?" You want to know about the Italians? Ah shuddup a ya face. Of course the granddaddy of the genre was Alf Garnett, stomping around in '*Til Death Do Us Part* railing against the 'coons' moving into the East End, before reappearing in *In Sickness and in Health* fighting a rearguard battle of wits and words with his carer – a large, gay black man. Although the writer Johnny Speight was using the character to satirise bigoted views, he had an uphill battle on his hands given the prevailing political climate. In a general election two years before Alf first appeared on TV screens, the Tories had poached the supposedly solid Labour seat of Smethwick thanks to their catchy slogan: "If you want a nigger for a neighbour, vote Labour."

While television used comedy to play out national tensions over immigration, on the football terraces the coping mechanism was more direct: aggressive ridicule. Following the arrival of the South Africans Gerry Francis and Albert Johanneson at Leeds United, a succession of black players were welcomed into top-flight English football with monkey chants and the odd carelessly-flung banana. Sadly, even Ron Atkinson, the man seen as a visionary for introducing the talents of Cyrille Regis, Brendon Batson and Laurie Cunningham into the West Bromwich Albion side of the mid-seventies, disgraced himself decades later by deriding Chelsea player Marcel Desailly as a "lazy, thick nigger" into a TV commentary microphone he had assumed was turned off. It was a sad day when Atkinson's racist outburst darkened football; he lost our respect, we lost the scattergun patois of gibberish he used to blast through televised games. Lollipops, going easy-oasy, dishing out spotter's badges, it lifted the commentary above the mundane. Who wants a near-post header when you can have fizzy eyebrows at the front stick?

Another question: whatever happened to the Dangerous Darkies? It sounds like the quintessential mid-seventies sitcom that never made it past pre-production. I can see them now, a couple of young bucks in kipper ties with extravagant afros, kicking around the back streets of the East End, obsessing about booze, birds and footie. But it is in fact the question I asked myself as I headed out of Limpopo the day after my meeting with Nelly.

Their story starts early in the last century in a British army base near the town of Nelspruit in the old Transvaal province. The soldiers had taken to filling their idle moments with a spot of association football and the garrison commander, trying to affirm an uneasy peace with the indigenous population, extended an invitation to a local team to come and give his chaps a gentle workout. An unpromising-looking rabble duly arrived and lined up against the army team. Well. If the British Empire was won on the playing fields of Eton, then it had its buttocks whipped as pink as the map on a corner of a foreign field that day. There is no record of the score, merely the reaction of the garrison commander as he watched quivering from the touchline. I can see him now: a ramrod straight figure in immaculately pressed khakis, sweating beneath a peaked cap, a nervous thumb and forefinger stroking a pencil moustache and occasionally replacing a fallen monocle. As his jaw tightens with the strain of repressed emotion he turns to his subaltern: "I say Binky, these darkies are a bit dangerous, what?" And so Mpumalanga's iconic team was born.

Unsurprisingly they had soon secured legendary status as the outfit that had taken on the old colonial masters and hoiked their pants down in grand style. In the days before widespread telecommunications the story passed by word of mouth and their myth burgeoned. The downside of this ephemeral existence is that there is little by way of documented evidence to explain what happened next. The fact that so many local clubs have assumed the name – Nelly's brother's side, the Majamela Dangerous Darkies, is just one of numerous examples I have stumbled across – is proof of the indelible mark left by the original talismen, but what became of them? They were the dominant club in the region, rose and fell between leagues, went through the usual upheavals over ownership and relocations, but then what? I asked Moses if he could shed any light.

"Eish, I know that club, they were tough guys; skilful, tricky players."

"Did you ever see them play?"

"No, I don't think so. They were up in the north, maybe they didn't come down to Gauteng much."

I had a similar response from other football fans I asked – the name and legendary exploits were well known, but further details were a bit thin. I began to wonder if the notion of the Dangerous Darkies was more important than the reality. Everything about them seems romantic, alluring and slightly mysterious. I found a website providing a database of global international football stadia that lists their home ground as the Stadium of Storms. It sounds wonderful, damned if I could find anyone who could place its whereabouts, mind you. Perhaps this elusive quality is just part of the attraction – providing the vital element of *fantasy* that stirs the hearts of South African football fans.

The game introduced to South Africa at the end of the 19th century by soldiers and missionaries was a fairly basic, unsophisticated beast – a lively hoof-about with elbows, knees and shoulders to the fore. As it spread to the backstreets of rapidly growing urban settlements, a new style emerged to cope with the demands of playing in restricted, confined spaces. Here, physical dominance paled against the ability to retain control of the ball. Like the young Pelé honing his craft dribbling a sock full of newspaper around the favelas of São Paulo, the stars of the township soon learnt how to keep the ball on a string. This in turn encouraged a culture of skill and showmanship as opponents were defeated at close quarters by a feint, shimmy, shibobo or tsamaya. This style was exhibited in its ephemeral perfection that searing afternoon in June 1970 at the Azteca Stadium, as the golden shirts of Brazil danced rings around the maddened, mesmerised Azzurri. If that sublime performance has a soundtrack it is surely the joyous, incessant thump of the samba drums. In his excellent book *Laduma! Soccer politics and society in South Africa*, Peter Alegi draws a similar line between the South African style of street play that developed decades ago and the dominant musical style beating relentlessly from the shibeens and dancehalls around that time: Marabi.

This free-form fusion of swing and jazz provided the soundtrack to social events stretching over entire weekends. A welcome escape from the drudgery of daily work and the overbearing influence of a controlling government, Marabi parties offered the chance to drink and dance your cares away. This flowing, carefree attitude soon found its way onto the makeshift football pitches of the backstreets.

In the 1930s an icy blast swept through football's hothouse, bringing a new ethos that was pragmatic and disciplined, one might even say dour. A succession of professional clubs from Scotland – notably Motherwell – had begun to tour South Africa and they imported novelties such as structure, formations and a neat passing game in which the ball did the running, not the man. Like anything new, the 'Motherwell style' soon caught the eyes of fans and the press. Suddenly the energy-sapping African game looked primitive – all huff and puff but no finesse; plenty of trickery but where's the end product? – and many teams began to experiment with a more regimented approach. This new wave left players and fans in a quandary. On the one hand they wanted to appear progressive, willing to explore new techniques and methods, on the other this European style of play seemed to distil the game down to its more functional elements. The sight of a ball zipping neatly between midfield triangles may have a certain geometric appeal, but it was much more fun watching your ace winger pop a shibobo between the legs of a defender, turn, and shimmy back for another go.

In essence it was time for South African football culture to face the question that burns at the heart of most sporting endeavours:

can we be successful *and* look good? Tough on opponents but easy on the eye? The answer is simple: yes. The caveat, equally so – but you need to be sublimely, breathtakingly talented. Consider the great West Indian cricketer Viv Richards. When *Wisden*, cricket's golden bible, named their five players of the last century Richards's broad grin beamed out from the front row. Like Pelé before him, Viv's schooling owed much to his basic surroundings – mastering the unruly bounce of a ball on a beach before smiting it into the sea with a piece of driftwood. His technique was drawn not from the MCC textbook but a manual he wrote himself. Ugly, rising deliveries that mortals would duck under or prod away with a defensive straight bat, Richards preferred to biff into the stand, often accompanied by a jaunty raise of the leg. Like the Brazilians in 1970 he exhibited a beautiful natural rhythm that, on its day, could play not just opponents, but the game itself, clean off the park. More Marabi than Motherwell.

It is clear that the Dangerous Darkies sit somewhere on the fine line between fantasy and reality – a wonderful team of yesteryear, slowly disappearing into the realms of myth. In an interview shortly after his side's opening match of the 2010 finals, Brazilian midfielder Gilberto Silva seemed to suggest that his predecessors from 1970 might be going the same way. Of course, there is the regularly revisited footage of that golden side as incontrovertible proof of their existence, but 40 years on are the 'legends' of that era edging ever closer to the literal definition of that word, are they now part of a romanticised or popularised myth of modern times? Gilberto seemed to think so: "Despite what some people expect, that Brazil will score four or five goals, people must know that football has changed. If you play a very open game you can have a problem at the end of the day."

There were some fantasy fans on show at Ellis Park for that first game – the orderly pocket of North Korean 'supporters' turned out to be a central casting hotchpotch of government stooges and

Chinese 'volunteers' – but the football was rooted firmly in reality. In fairness it's not easy to conjure up snaky-hipped samba skills when you're swathed in thermal underwear. Despite the chilly conditions, when the goals arrived they had the warm glow of Brazilian quality. Maicon's shot from a hopeless angle swerved so luxuriously that it immediately hung the jury between fluke and yet more mischief from Jabulani. Robinho's slide-rule pass across the box to set up Elano for the second was a masterpiece of weighted precision. Unlike Pelé's stylishly laconic lay-off to Carlos Alberto, where the beauty lay in the apparent casualness of the execution.

Poor old Brazil. While other national sides carry the burden of expectant home support, it often feels like the Esquadrão de Ouro are responsible for shaping the feel of the whole tournament. After the opening week in South Africa the chuntering was audible: bore draws, insufficient goals, a lack of dead-ball theatrics. The officials had been good, great in fact, but one isn't supposed to notice that. If the mood was to be lifted, at some point Brazil would need to step up. At least history was on their side.

Dazzled to the sidelines after 1970 by the orange glow of total football, the Brazilians returned with a vengeance in 1982 as players like Zico, Júnior and Sócrates stole the show. Modern elite sport considers every detail in the search for an advantage – diet, lifestyle, specially-designed kit. Consider Sócrates. A qualified doctor who presumably skipped the classes on sclerosis and lung cancer – he enjoyed a drink and smoked like a chimney. His hair was wildly exuberant, his shorts tiny. Everything seemed stacked against optimum sporting performance, yet there he was waltzing through opposing defences, sliding the ball past their keeper. The show-stopper in Spain was the match against Italy. Brazil only needed a draw but could not suppress their instinct to pour forward, setting up some wonderful helter-skelter mayhem that eventually shuddered to a halt leaving them 2-3 losers.

By the turn of the 1990s the policy was shifting – out with

flamboyance and flair, in with pugnacity and pragmatism. The new approach was built around Dunga. Nick-named after Dopey from the Seven Dwarfs, the midfield general was anything but. Snapping and snarling, breaking up the play, he personified the ethos of the 1994 champions – defensive solidity first; the odd goal poached here and there. His side equalled the fewest number of goals scored by a World Cup victor. An exhausting 0-0 spread over two hours in the broiling heat of the Pasadena Rose Bowl dragged the final towards a sad denouement from the penalty spot. Dunga lifted the trophy, Baresi and Baggio, two of the star men of the tournament, carried the can home to Italy.

As Dunga the coach led his men into battle at the 2010 tournament, Sócrates was unequivocal about the direction he saw Brazil heading in: "Brazil are boring. The players in the national team are chained by this pragmatism. I hope that some of them can break from the leash and remember that priceless memories and conquests in football include putting smiles on people's faces.

"I like to see myself as a philosopher of the game, and what can be better than to think of football as the only sport that allows so much lack of regularity? Dunga is not to blame for what is going on in Brazilian football – he is a victim. It doesn't matter who is the manager, because other guys would also be adopting the same style, because that's what the establishment wants.

"They have been winning tournaments and games but the team lacks a player who embodies the true free spirit of Brazilian football."

Watching the yellow shirts of Bafana Bafana chasing Uruguayan shadows en route to a 3-0 defeat in Pretoria, Carlos Alberto Parreira must have had very different feelings – a weighty nostalgia for the defensive solidity of his 1994 golden boys. Mexico's subsequent defeat of an uninspired France the following evening strongly suggested the hosts would be leaving their own party earlier than hoped. World Cup boss Danny Jordaan didn't mince his words:

"I hope that Bafana Bafana's slaughtering on the field last night is also in the name of future hope. Last night the team just couldn't get into first gear. This was a hugely disappointing night for South Africa and it left the tournament in pain."

Looking at the Bafana fans drifting to the exits in the latter stages of the Uruguay game, I wondered where they might transfer their loyalties. Any sort of England run would attract a following – the Premier League is obsessively followed in South Africa, the townships are a museum of vintage shirts: Liverpool, Man United, Arsenal. A lively showing from the Dutch could stir some interest, notwithstanding a possibly antipathy to cheering the orange flag. In actual fact, the answer was right in front of me, in the golden shirts of the local fans trudging out of the Loftus Versfeld Stadium. When it's not hosting big rugby fixtures for the Bulls, Loftus accommodates the Brazilians of South African football – Mamelodi Sundowns.

A pillar of the original Gauteng football community, Sundowns hit the jackpot in 2004 when mining magnate Patrice Motsepe, a rand billionaire, bought the club. Back-to-back Premier League titles followed, mirroring the success that Chelsea enjoyed shortly after Roman Abramovich poured a slick of oil money into the club. The similarities end there. Two of the deepest dips into Abramovich's bottomless barrel of cash saw a pair of African gems – Essien and Drogba – imported to London. At Sundowns around that time one of their biggest names was Peter Ndlovu – a Zimbabwean winger with a headless chicken dribbling style that had stirred a flutter of excitement at Coventry City back in the nineties. I was amazed to rediscover him still playing, a generation later, masquerading as a star turn. But maybe I should not have been. With the talent on their doorstep spirited away it is little wonder that the African leagues depend on youthful talent and faded former stars.

Known locally as 'the Brazilians', Sundowns play in yellow shirts, blue shorts and white socks and have historically aspired to playing a beautiful game, thanks in part to the legacy of their coach Stanley 'Screamer' Tshabalala. His *tiki tiki* style demanded a game played at a high tempo but without sacrificing style – a philosophy Sócrates and his team of 1982 clearly approved of.

A slight linguistic variation, it was *Tic Tac* that carried Spain into the tournament on a high, challenging Brazil for the title of favourites. The *rápido* pass and move style that won Euro 2008 and helped Barcelona sweep aside Manchester United in the Champions League Final the following year inspired fear ahead of the tournament. They looked unstoppable. That was until the opening game when the Swiss nudged them aside 1-0 courtesy of a goal redolent of Wimbledon FC in their late 1980s pomp – an unruly goalmouth bundle resolved by an angry punt into the net. So much for style over substance.

I WAS DRIVING FROM LIMPOPO INTO MPUMALANGA HEADING FOR Nelspruit, on the trail of the Dangerous Darkies, dropping down into the Lowveld, South Africa's northern garden; a land of plenty. Miles of lush, prosperous farmlands full of carefully-ordered fruit groves bursting with mangoes, pawpaws, naartjies and bananas spread away from the banks of the Sabie River. In the distance, tea plantations clung to the foothills of the Drakensberg Mountains. This was a landscape in which almost anything could grow and flourish. Except, it would seem, football.

Back in Limpopo, Black Leopards, the only team from the province represented in the Premier League, were sliding towards the First Division. Waiting to meet them were their neighbours Dynamos, another fallen giant. As for Mpumalanga, after the demise of the Dangerous Darkies, the only other club with any real standing, the Mpumalanga Black Aces, provide a case study for the confused evolutions of a South African football club. In 1998 Giant Aces became Pietersburg Pillars when a businessman from Limpopo (then the Northern Province) relocated them to Pietersburg (now Polokwane) to compete in the First Division (subsequently renamed the Mvela league, now the *National* First Division). The club was then bought by Robson Mongwe, a Limpopo funeral parlour mogul, who changed the name to City Pillars and appointed former Orlando Pirates striker Jerry 'Legs of Thunder' Sikhosana as player-manager. Mongwe then sold the club franchise to the Cypriot businessman Laki Morfou, whose son Mario had played for Witbank Black Aces in the late 1990s. Laki re-relocated the club back to its former province and changed the name to Mpumalanga Black Aces. Simple as that.

To further confuse things, as the northern provinces are home to the Kruger National Park, the phrase 'beautiful game' carries an entirely different meaning up there. Spread over 7,332 square miles, the Kruger is the largest game reserve in South Africa, offering its 1.3m annual visitors the chance to see The Big Five (lion, elephant, buffalo, leopard and rhinoceros) as well as giraffe, cheetah, hippo and many other wild and beautiful things. A happy marriage of conservation and commerce, the daily entrance fee of R132 rises to an eye-watering R15,000 per night for the most exclusive lodges.

Speeding alongside the wire fence marking its perimeter, the more basic realities of the local economy were very much in evidence. Either side of the small settlements we drove through, human traffic rolled alongside the road on a dusty track. Lean, bare-chested men, bent over wheelbarrows and other makeshift trolleys, were urging jumbles of sticks and jagged metal along, swaying from side to side with the exertion. By contrast, the women in brightly patterned traditional dresses were a study in poise and grace. Centred by the bulky sacks of fruit or laundry balanced on their heads, they glided onwards with spines as straight as broom handles.

Every so often a tree spreading shade across the roadside provided an opportunity for walkers to rest or set out their wares for sale. In such an unforgiving climate shade is a valuable commodity and, as such, it tends to follow the money. Take a drive around the wealthier suburbs of Johannesburg nestling in the city heights, and marvel at the density of the surrounding foliage. The hyperbole of estate agents is legendary – how we cheered when our warzone in Hackney became 'Homerton Village', after the local kebab shop risked a table and chairs on the pavement and the council repainted the zebra crossing – but even they would have to do better than 'leafy' to describe certain streets in Johannesburg. 'Rainforesty' would be nearer the mark. Driving along these broad avenues is like taking a diversion via Middle Earth, with little or no sunlight permeating the bottle green canopy pressing down from above. By contrast, on the outskirts of the city, the ramshackle dwellings of the township are left exposed to the heat and glare of the sun. Here, in place of trees to soften the skyline, all that rises from the ground are the municipal streetlights; four bulbs mounted on towering stalks that instantly put one in mind of a prison camp.

The town of Nelspruit rose suddenly and quite incongruously in the distance. Set in a bed of arable fertility, surrounded by the ragged edges of the mountains, the shimmering glass of office blocks looked futuristic, but in a backward kind of way. I bypassed the city centre and followed the highway out of town, heading for the site of the new Mbombela Stadium.

Nelspruit, like Polokwane, faced the daunting challenge of building a new stadium from scratch. But even before the foundation stones were laid, cracks began to appear in the billion-rand project. Early in 2007 the project manager was sacked by the Municipality amidst rumours of irregularities in the process of awarding the lucrative construction contracts. Just as the dust appeared to be settling on this media storm, the land itself became an issue.

The site of the Mbombela lies within a 6,000ha plot returned to a local family, the Mdluli clan, in 2003 under the terms of the Land Restitution Act. The legal title passed to the Matsafeni Trust, and the Trustees sold a parcel of land to the Municipality to build the stadium, for a single rand. The beneficiaries of the Trust had supposedly been promised jobs on the site in return, but rumours of a private business arrangement between the Trust and the Municipality aroused enough suspicion to encourage the beneficiaries to bring a class action against the Trustees. In 2009 a settlement was reached whereby the Municipality agreed to pay the Trust R8.7m to confirm their title to the land housing the new stadium. Pursuing a separate claim, the Nkosi family, another local clan, filed papers with the Land Claims Office challenging the Mdluli's title to the entire plot, asserting ownership rights as the original occupants of the farmlands who had been evicted by the previous white owners. As if all that wasn't enough, almost from day one the building works were dogged by an unrelenting series of strikes over safety, conditions and pay.

The stadium is set back from the highway down a path leading through forestland. There was little of note to see – men with diggers kicking up dust in the shadow of a giant, grey Lego set – but the artist's impression of the finished article looked impressive. As is often the case with these projections into the future the placard depicted a homogenised, 1950s-style utopia – men in pressed suits reading newspapers, children flying box kites, mothers pushing canopied prams – in which everyone grins with helpless delirium.

I wondered what the future really held for this vast monolith stirring in the forests, a few miles out of town. To appease political sensitivities the 2010 organising committee decided to spread the games thinly across the country – ensuring that every province (except the sparsely populated Northern Cape) was served a slice of the action. Polokwane and Nelspruit faced rising costs, restive workers and land ownership disputes against the backdrop of a national energy crisis, as they battled to deliver two state-of-the-art stadiums on schedule. And for what? The northern venues only hosted a handful of games in the first stage of the tournament after which the serious business of the knockout competition settled in

Johannesburg, Port Elizabeth, Cape Town and Durban. When a gleaming new stadium was built for the 2002 Commonwealth Games in Manchester, shortly after the closing ceremony Manchester City FC and their army of fans moved in. With no major teams in either Limpopo or Mpumalanga to seduce local fans away from the charms of Chiefs and Pirates (or, for that matter, Manchester United and Barcelona), I wondered how the new grounds would get the use that they deserved and the huge investment merited.

The rough sandy track leading through the forest to the Mbombela was lined by an avenue of eucalyptus trees, their pale grey trunks and sage-coloured leaves catching sunlight dappled through the surrounding forest. The rumble of mechanised and human toil drifted out of earshot and soon the only sound I could hear was the metronomic crunch of my footsteps. To my right, through the trees, I spotted a pair of rusty goal frames sitting at either end of a patchy stretch of grass. Suddenly the calm was broken by a cacophony of excited noise as a group of schoolchildren spilled across the field. They joined me on the path – running, dancing, shouting, chasing – heading for home. One little girl with closely cropped hair, huge dark eyes and a golden ring through each earlobe skipped alongside me for a while, blowing a rooty-tooty tune through the blades of grass cupped in her hands.

"Nice vuvuzela," I said, puffing out my cheeks and wiggling my fingers over an invisible trumpet in what I imagined to be a comical fashion.

She smiled politely, and skipped away. Her school, set further back beyond the path, neighboured the new stadium development and I wondered how much of the colour, excitement and fervour of the World Cup would permeate that little life. I was still trying to understand how the resources being poured in to this clearing in the woods would really benefit local people, and decided to look for some answers in town.

I managed to find the Nelspruit branch of SAFA and was soon shaking hands with a man sitting on a stool outside a travel agency in the centre of town. This was Reuben Mahlalela, president of the local branch of SAFA, and someone who had been involved in football administration in the region for over thirty years. I followed Reuben into a small office, in which a few faded team photos and the odd curling press cutting sellotaped to the wall offered the only clues as to the work that went on there. He settled into a black leather armchair behind his desk and asked me what I wanted to know.

I asked how he felt the 2010 preparations were progressing in Nelspruit. Reuben leant back, closed his eyes and talked me through a series of deadlines and targets, none of which were providing him with any genuine cause for concern. He had the kind of wise, venerable aura that would need more than a few labour and land ownership disputes to shift. He referred to a recent visit to South Africa by Sepp Blatter, and the complimentary, reassuring comments that had subsequently emerged from Fifa concerning the health of the 2010 project. He also observed that during a recent interview Blatter had discussed the benefits of artificial pitches, suggesting that 2010 may be a logical opportunity to showcase their merits and value.

I launched into a pompous, ill-informed diatribe about the Americanisation of football, the sanctity of the World Cup and how using synthetic pitches would be like taking a sledgehammer to the already crumbling foundations of a once proud game. Something like that. It was only a small office but I somehow managed to mount my high horse and take it for a brisk canter around the filing cabinets. Once I had dismounted, Reuben talked quietly about the difficulties of maintaining the pitch at the Mbombela in such a climate – securing the necessary water supply alone presented a serious logistical issue. He went on to explain how, if the stadium had a more resilient man-made covering, it could be used for a variety of functions – social and cultural events, political gatherings, markets – providing the community with a multi-purpose space for many years. Not for the first time I realised that I'm an idiot. An hour earlier I had been wandering through the woods with the schoolchildren, fretting about the negligible value that 2010 would bring to their community. But at the first suggestion that something as prosaic as reality might besmirch my glossy, Westernised ideal of a football tournament, I had reared up in horror.

As I travelled the country talking to people about 2010 the 'L' word cropped up time and again: legacy. Once the party was over and the guests had returned home, how would this gleaming new infrastructure benefit not only the football fraternities in South Africa but also the communities that sustain them? At least in Mpumalanga it seemed that the organisers had a realistic eye on the future.

A huge man walked in and introduced himself as Patson Mashele, another local executive for SAFA. He had soon disabused me of the notion that the province was a footballing wilderness. Mpumalanga may lack significant representation in the top flight, but below that the potential appears huge: 16 teams in the Vodacom League (effectively the third division), a further 36 in the SAB league and then over 350 sides battling to elevate themselves up from the Metropolitan Divisions. It seemed the region was alive with competition – a stunning venue like the new Mbombela would provide the perfect stage on which to pursue and realise aspirations; it could truly become a theatre of dreams. When I asked about the Dangerous Darkies, smiles and knowing glances were exchanged.

"Those guys walloped everybody," said Reuben. "That was the danger: you played the Dangerous Darkies, you got walloped."

"But what happened to them, where did they go?" I asked.

"There were internal politics, problems within the management," he said with a weary sigh. "Sometimes it gets to the stage where people are not working in good faith."

A young man called Simon entered the office and offered to

show me around while Reuben and Patson talked. In truth this really only involved walking further down the corridor to look at another office adorned with press cuttings providing a potted history of local triumphs. A tall, slim figure with an elegant Grecian profile, Simon was an eloquent, impressive young man. He explained that he was volunteering at SAFA but that his real interest was in establishing a tourism business. He had recognised the potential of 2010 tours that offered access to both kinds of game and was looking to find some sponsors. We had been talking for about five minutes when another young man entered the room and Simon made the introductions. I'm afraid his real name didn't stick, but for reasons that will become clear, to me he will be forever Eric. He was also volunteering at SAFA and was working with Simon in his tourism ventures. Otherwise the pair were chalk and cheese. While Simon was tall and thin, calm and measured, Eric was a tubby little barrel of nonsense, bouncing off the walls with excitement as he described how they were going to clean up.

"Eh, Reech I'm telling you, *pounds*, that's what we like here." He rubbed his thumb and forefinger together inches from my face, grinning with delight. He nodded at Simon. "This guy, eish, he's clever man; numbers and figures, it's no problem." He took a few steps back and placed his palms on his chest. "And me, you know what I do?"

I shook my head.

"Sales and marketing, *say-els and mar - keee - teng*." He physically stretched each word out in the air as if pulling at an invisible chest expander.

"So sell me a holiday in Nelspruit," I said.

Eric beamed, shot me with a pistol finger, spun on his heel and strode to the farthest corner of the room. He then turned to face me and made his way slowly back to where he had started, sauntering across the room with a laconic, devil-may-care look on his face. He grabbed a chair, spun it around and sat on it backwards – a tad hastily judging by the slight wince he gave on landing. Leaning on the back of the chair he settled his chins into a 'v' between his thumb and forefinger, and eyed me thoughtfully.

"My friend, you look like a man that enjoys the good things in life. You like football? We got the World Cup – *the We-e-eld Cup* – right here. You want to see some wild animals? No problem – the Kruger Park is just over there – go on a drive, see the Big Five; it's beautiful man, trust me. Now then…" He eased himself carefully off the chair and took a few steps in my direction. "…you like entertainment?"

I nodded, slowly. He came closer, to within a few inches, and looked up at me, a conspiratorial grin bulging across his chubby chops.

"We got braais and drinks by the pool, we got nightlife, dancing."

He was now leaning on me and I could feel the unmistakable sensation of an elbow exploring my ribcage.

"We got everything you need here, my friend."

Now his eyebrows were getting in on the act, rising and falling in time with the jabbing elbow.

"Eh? Eh? Do you know what I mean? Do you know what I mean?"

Suddenly I was back in 1970s comedy-land: nudge, nudge, wink, wink, say no more. But he did.

"I have three words for you, my friend: cheeks and cherries." He raised his thumb and forefinger and kissed them: "*Che-e-eeks and che-e-e-rries.*"

I looked up at Simon, standing quietly in the far corner of the room, grinning helplessly. I popped my head around the office door and said goodbye to Reuben, wishing the president good luck with the challenges that lay ahead. He nodded and smiled, a calm reassuring presence. Not long after I returned from my trip I learnt that he had passed away after a short illness. Sadly this man who spent his life working to bring the game to this remote corner of the country was not there when the world of football arrived.

Driving back to Johannesburg I wondered how the World Cup would reach out and touch the people scattered throughout this landscape of farmlands and game reserves. At first glance the dozing bulk lying in the forest at Mbombela had looked suspiciously like a white elephant. But my subsequent conversations with the guys at SAFA had reassured me that there was enough action in the local area – football or otherwise – to give life to the new stadium.

In the end the Mbombela, a stadium stuck out in the wilds, witnessed a team from football's backwoods unseat the world champions. But somehow Italy 1 – New Zealand 1 didn't quite have the same magic as the turnovers that Cameroon and Senegal visited upon Argentina and France respectively in past tournaments. There was a lack of romance – the Kiwis stuck to a solid men-behind-the-ball game plan, the Italians struggled to shift out of their native caution and force the issue. Defenders vied for the man of the match award.

Watching Inter Milan win the Champions League Final a month before the World Cup kicked off, building success upon a defensive rockery hewn from Brazilian granite, I remembered my conversation with Reuben about the artificial pitches and glowed with shame. I recalled his quiet, measured words, emphasising the need for a realistic approach if the World Cup was to really secure longer-term benefits for the wider community. I realised that my self-righteous reaction had stemmed from a desire to have a World Cup that lived up to *my* expectations – ideally one in which Brazil took the tournament by storm, vanquishing opponents with mesmeric style, breathtaking trickery and a volley of wonder goals. I didn't want plastic pitches and the reliable solidity of Gilberto Silva – I wanted a soft green carpet and the lunacy of Sócrates.

Above all I wanted what we all crave but can never have – a World Cup that lives up to the rose-tinted memories of our first.

A TALE OF TWO CITIES

IT WAS THE BEST OF GAMES, IT WAS THE WORST OF GAMES, IT was the season of Light, it was the season of Darkness, it was the spring of hope, it was the winter of despair, we had everything before us, we had nothing before us.

Steven Gerrard, honouring a contractual obligation to face the cameras shortly after England's goalless draw with Algeria, threw a blanket of blame over all concerned: "It was their World Cup Final." The subtext was arrogant but accurate. The North Africans were up against a team 22 places above them in the Fifa hierarchy – former world champions whose clubs dominated Europe and whose star names stood alongside the greatest in the history of the game. For the Algerians, England at the Green Point Stadium would be their biggest, best game of the tournament, their World Cup Final. So, yes, go on then Stevie, the best of games for Algeria.

The worst of games for England? Looking at recent World Cup history, the competition amongst second game stinkers is pretty fierce – the draw with the Morrocans in 1986 takes some licking, as does 82 minutes of deadlock with Trinidad and Tobago twenty years later. So this was not unfamiliar territory – or was it? Tireless endeavour going unrewarded we know well, but against the Algerians there was something else afoot. After the game a number of pundits pointed the finger at Capello. He was too stern, too detached from the players – they were playing with *fear*, locked into a system he demanded, unable to express themselves on or off the pitch. Ironically this same approach had earned the Italian high praise during the celebrated qualifying campaign – the grizzled old disciplinarian had shocked our pampered players into a run of

---

consistent performances. He could do no wrong.

The US game had been disappointing but the manager's authority remained certain – you only had to listen to his response to Franz Beckenbauer's suggestion that England were resorting to "kick and rush", whereas if you'd watched Germany dismantle the Australians… "They played a good game when they played eleven against ten," observed Fabio dryly, leaving precious little lost in translation.

So what had happened to the players? They left an English spring bathed in a warm glow of expectation; two weeks later, caught in the middle of an African winter, they looked frozen, rigid with fear. Were they really inhibited by the coach, was he living up to the 'Don Fabio' image? Forget about it.

"I hope, when we play the next game, we forget this performance and we forget to play with fear and without confidence."

Much of the debate in the days leading up to the game had focussed around questions of confidence in the goalkeeper. After days of wild speculation, shortly before the players stepped onto the team bus, David James got the nod, leaving Robert Green writhing in purgatory, unable to atone for his earlier sin. To an extent, England's new No1 set the tone for the evening. A ball looped in from the Algerian right flank, James advanced – a dominant, physical presence – but rather than collect it he caught the Jabulani with a mighty uppercut, sending it on a steep vertical trajectory. It came to earth near Gareth Barry who swung his boot but only managed a slice that sent the ball spinning invitingly across the England penalty box from where it was hoofed back up the pitch. This little vignette of mishaps and misjudgements was replayed all over the field on a night when England struggled to find any sort of rhythm or poise.

Usually with disappointing performances there are one or two key moments to look back on and ponder what might have been – if x had buried that chance, if y had not been sent off. But that was the curious thing about the Algeria game – the England performance was utterly nondescript: sure there were no heroes, but there wasn't even an obvious scapegoat.

A tournament that was already under duress for its lack of quality and mean goals quota didn't need England 0 Algeria 0; it left quite a stench – fortunately, the following evening the Denmark and Cameroon players cracked a window, ushering in a breath of fresh air. Unsung past champions from their respective continents, travelling to South Africa without excess baggage – just quiet intent – they were a good match. By contrast England v Algeria had the whiff of a blood sport – a possible giant-killing was on the cards; inequality was the unavoidable sub-plot, which made Cape Town the ideal hunting ground.

The city's premier football team Ajax Cape Town is, as the name suggests, a franchise of the Amsterdam club. How, you might ask, does a football power on the edge of central Europe colonise a club at the tip of Africa? The anwser lies somewhere along the football food chain; let's start with the 1995 Champions League Final.

The meeting in Vienna brought together the once and future kings of European football. Appearing in their third consecutive final, AC Milan wore the crown, still strutting after their 4-0 demolition of Barcelona the previous year. Boasting elegance, guile, muscle and invention, the Rossoneri of Maldini, Baresi, Desailly and Boban looked unstoppable. Standing in their path was an Ajax side ready to test the shortly to be announced theory that "you'll win nothing with kids".

Despite having an average age of 23, the likes of Seedorf, Davids, Overmars, Kanu and the De Boer twins defied the odds, playing without fear, holding the Italian giants at bay. In the dying moments of the game Ajax veteran Frank Rijkaard threaded a pass between his former Milanese teammates to set up Patrick Kluivert for the *coup de grace*. Ajax's reappearance in the final the following year confirmed the suspicion that this young side would go on to rule Europe for the next decade. But of course they did not.

AC Milan have a habit of snapping up their tormentors. After Paolo Di Canio's peach of a goal for Napoli floored the reds towards the end of their 1994 Serie A campaign, they immediately sought his signature. There was only so long they could sit and watch Juve's Roberto Baggio run rings round them before employing his services. Having let Ruud Gullit join Sampdoria for the 1993/94 season they bought him back after he slammed home the winner in Samp's 3-2 victory over his old teammates. True to form, a year after their Viennese nightmare, il Diavolo ripped the heart out of the young Ajax side. Well, perhaps the spine is more anatomically correct: Reiziger and Bogarde from the back, the midfield general Davids and, of course, Kluivert at the sharp end. All gobbled up by the football food chain.

Working from the assumption that history + glamour x money = status, we might find the food chain working something like this: Real Madrid, Manchester United, Barcelona, Milan – other perennial Champions League contenders – the best of the rest of the Premiership, La Liga and Serie A – the rest of Western Europe – South America – Eastern Europe – Africa. Apart from the odd curve ball like Beckham's move to LA Galaxy, this seems a reasonable sketch of the pecking order. If we sit Ajax somewhere around the upper mid-point we see them looking up to Milan at the top table, but peering far down to the crumbs around the floor – at the kind of clubs that might be willing to hand their choicest morsels back to their master.

IF YOU TAKE A WALK IN THE HILLS ABOVE CAPE TOWN, nosing through the sandy pathways and shady pines of Newlands Forest, you will eventually arrive at a clearing permitting a panoramic view of the city, the *whole city*. To your far left the city bowl – with beaches and bays, boardwalks and malls – is small but perfectly formed, a beautiful town nestled in the warm embrace of Table

Mountain and Lion's Head. As your eyes pan right, away from the glass and chrome of the CBD, the skyline levels, stretching away for mile upon mile of shacks: the Cape Flats.

At one extreme, driving the coast road around from Sea Point to Hout Bay, one passes multi-million rand real estate clinging to the cliffs above the froth and spume of the Indian Ocean. Head out through the city centre towards the airport, cruising down the N2 past endless shacks tumbling to the edge of the highway, and you will eventually reach the other extreme: Khayelitsha, a vast township creeping further into the bush as new arrivals build their shacks on sand shifting in the stiff sea breezes. This is Cape Town's food chain, and it's a long journey from one end to the other.

Looking down on this from Newlands Forest a landmark rises signifying, in a very crude sense, the midway point. Within sight of the city suburbs of Woodstock and Mowbray one way and the formal townships of Langa and Belgravia the other, a pair of industrial cooling towers sit by the N2; this is Athlone and it was there, a decade ago, that I caught my first sight of South African football.

There was a whiff of revolution in the air that evening at the old Athlone Stadium, a rather tired brick and corrugated iron structure. The news had broken that Cape Town's two leading clubs were to merge under the banner of Ajax Cape Town – adopting the badge and club colours of the Amsterdam giant. The stadium was hosting a double bill of matches that night. First up Cosmos took on Cape Town Spurs. I headed down to the bowels of the stadium, muttered "BBC" to the steward guarding the tunnel and wandered out on to the turf. I had been commissioned by *Match of the Day Magazine* to write a piece about football in South Africa to acknowledge their recent World Cup debut and stated aspiration to host the tournament in 2006. I wandered around the pitch clutching an ancient, borrowed SLR camera sporting a vast zoom lens. I imagined it leant me an authentic journalistic air. Thunder rumbled overhead and soon the rain was teeming down. Watching the highlights later that evening I caught glimpses of myself, prowling the touchline, occasionally dropping to one knee to fire off a clutch of action shots. Even through the wobbly TV footage and sheeting rain you could tell I was an old hand, leaving the lens cap on to keep out the weather.

On the touchline opposite me stood the stout figure of Jomo Sono, a plastic chair above his head. Above him the grandstand was a dark mass of humanity. I took a couple more Zen photographs and headed for shelter. Steaming on the terrace, the warmth of the occasion enveloped me. There were the families enjoying a long evening of football: clucking matrons dishing out bunny chow and prego rolls to boisterous children who just wanted to chase their friends up and down the steps. Groups of young guys clustered in the shadows welcomed the weekend with surreptitious dops from brown paper bags. Dagga smoke rose to the undulations of the corrugated iron roof. There were cheerful greetings and insults, horns hooting, sirens wailing. The football wasn't great – odd flashes of brilliance from some young, unpolished diamonds – but the atmosphere was wonderful.

There was a definite sense of purpose and positivity sweeping through South African football at that time. During the previous 12 months Jomo had guided Bafana to a second consecutive African Nations Cup Final, cementing their place as one of the Dark Continent's leading lights. They then travelled to France for a useful debut World Cup; two draws and a defeat to the eventual champions promised better things to come.

My piece for the magazine reported this growing sense of upward mobility; the cover of that issue featured another young footballing force coming to terms with great expectations: David Beckham. Vilified from all sides for his part in England's dismissal in France at the hands of Argentina – *The Mirror* went with "10 Heroic Lions, One Stupid Boy", the terraces strung up effigies and bellowed boos – by the spring of 1999 brand Beckham was risking a relaunch.

Allow me to creak open the cupboard of footballing cliché and point out that at this time England were in the market for a player who could take a game by the scruff of its neck, stand up and be counted, roll his sleeves up and dig in, take their game to the next level. At the end of the day, to be fair, Beckham seemed to be the man for the job.

Another master of the mangled metaphor –"I'm looking for players to hit me in the eye and nail a shirt" – Glenn Hoddle had recently, unexpectedly, removed Gazza, England's talisman of the past decade, from the international scene, nudging him closer to the edge of a darkening abyss. Shearer followed after Euro 2000, hoping to save the rest of his best for the Magpies. Another Toon legend, Kevin Keegan, added to the sense of uncertainty, hopping out of the managerial hot seat soon after. With the ship rudderless and listing, Beckham took on the job of skipper.

By the time his last-minute free kick against Greece had secured qualification for the 2002 World Cup, he was back as the darling of the tabloids: the "stupid boy" had grown some goldenballs. The quadrennial cycle was completed when England sunk Argentina in the Sapporo Dome, thanks to a penalty from the captain. As in disaster, the tabloid reaction in triumph was measured and thoughtful. "Up Yours Señors", boomed *The Sun*.

At Athlone that evening I was catching a last glimpse of the old order. A few months later when the season ended the local clubs Seven Stars and Cape Town Spurs disappeared for ever, lost as separate entities, reborn under the Ajax banner. The Amsterdam giant has similar arrangements with other clubs around the world but only in Cape Town are the name and colours adopted to create a true franchise. This willing surrender of identity and sovereignty came at a price. An astute agrarian nation, the Dutch nurture their seeds and saplings; to Ajax the land surrounding Cape Town looked fertile. During the off-season hundreds of youngsters from the nearby townships headed for the stadium, hoping to earn a place on the new Ajax scholarship programme to lift them up and away from the grim reality of everyday life. The best would make their way north to Amsterdam; the best of these may, in time, continue their odyssey to Milan, Manchester, Madrid. Interestingly, the most high-profile success story from this youth development project to date is Benni McCarthy, already ripe for the picking when the Dutch arrived. Brought up in the notorious Hanover Park district, McCarthy began with Seven Stars, was signed by Cape Town Spurs and then effectively rejoined his old club when the two merged under the Ajax badge. After a season in Amsterdam he moved on to Celta Vigo in Spain and then to Porto to spearhead the José Mourinho revolution.

Thirty years before this acquisition in the futures market, Cape Town Spurs had emerged to satisfy a basic demand. When an attempt to form a non-racial professional league – the People's League – began to develop in the mid-sixties, the footballing communities of Johannesburg had Pirates and Swallows, Durban had Bucks and Aces – South Africa's other major city needed a team. Hellenic were the leading lights, but they played in the white NFL.

By the mid 1970s the NFL had reached its peak and was able to attract some stellar names from the English game. During the 1974 season Hellenic, managed by Johnny 'Budgie' Byrne, fielded a team including Bobby Moore, Gordon Banks and Jeff Astle against a Jewish Guild XI featuring a guest appearance from George Best. A larger-than-life character, Byrne had made his name with Crystal Palace at the turn of the sixties. In 1962 he was called up to the England squad while Palace were still stuck in the Third Division, akin to Capello plucking someone from Yeovil Town to lead the line in South Africa.

Decades before nutritionists and dieticians were part of the coaching staff, the players looked after themselves; win or lose, on the booze – pints could be sweated off on the training pitch. This culture grated with the buttoned-up regime instilled by England's manager Alf Ramsey. Byrne enjoyed a drink and a laugh – he picked up the tag 'Budgie' for his incessant chatter – and his copybook was soon stained. Away from home on international duty, an evening curfew was missed; the following day as the players assembled in their blazers to meet local dignitaries, it was Budgie's elbow that sent Greavsie tumbling into the hotel pool. Neither man got his chance in 1966. Greaves was stuck to the bench, Byrne was cut when the training squad was reduced to the tournament 22. Like Gazza in 1998, this rejection presaged a slow descent as injury and drink took their toll. Byrne rejoined the Eagles, moved west to Fulham, then made the long migration south to Durban United, before landing the job at Hellenic and coaxing his illustrious former England colleagues down for a season in the Cape Town sun.

While the NFL was fielding fantasy pub sides, the People's League was slipping quietly under the table. The inflexible Pass laws and restricted access to playing grounds made it increasingly difficult for black players and administrators to organise their matches. Apartheid's grip was tightening as communities were divided and segregated. In a busy warren of streets perched on the hills above the centre of Cape Town one community had other ideas. Here was a place for diversity and togetherness; here was a rich melting pot of races and religions, of talent: professional, artistic and sporting, here you would find life in all its myriad forms. Here was District 6.

If you were to draw a timeline following the rise and fall of Apartheid, somewhere around the mid-point a cluster of events marks a slow turning of the tide; the point at which the true colours of this regime fluttered before a shocked world. These events are the Sharpeville Massacre, the Soweto Uprising and the forced removals from District 6.

Before the World Cup kicked off, I spent a day with Colleen, family friend, tour guide and former resident of the place formally christened the Sixth District of the Cape Town Municipality. We began in Green Point, a stone's throw from the new stadium. .

In this part of town hotels and apartment blocks run along the coastline, gazing out at the endless crystalline waters at the meeting point of the Indian and Atlantic Oceans. Further back, houses climb the foothills of Signal Hill, becoming grander as the view improves, following the generally safe principle that wealth rises. We pulled up next to the Green Point Track. There was not much to see – an old racing green wooden stand – but this was once a Mecca for non-white sport in Cape Town. The Track hosted athletics meetings, rugby and football matches, festivals and community events, picnics and family gatherings.

For many years the Track sat in the shadow of the old Green Point Stadium, a multipurpose venue boasting a proper running track, floodlights and surrounding grandstands. Colleen explained that this venue had been off-limits to non-whites, except for Thursdays when the coloured school was permitted access. The stadium was demolished and in its place the magnificent new arena rose. From the start the project was controversial as the residents of the nearby suburbs of Green Point and Sea Point – white, moneyed, middle-classes (not your average South African football fans) – objected forcefully to this imposition.

We drove into the centre of town and parked in front of The Castle. The points of this pentagonal stronghold represent the five principalities of Orange – a legacy of the Dutch mission that preceded the Ajax project. In 1652 Jan van Riebeeck arrived to set up a supply post for passing traders on behalf of the Dutch East India Company. Van Riebeeck needed labour but he was prohibited from enslaving the Khoi-San, the indigenous population. Slaves were imported from the colonies – Sumatra, Indonesia, Malaysia – or poached from passing hulks. During a period of emancipation in

Highs and lows for the Bafana Republic: the fantasy of Shabba's screamer
is followed by the harsh reality of an early exit

God save the team – Rooney seeks divine inspiration…
while in Rosemoor a young fan keeps the faith

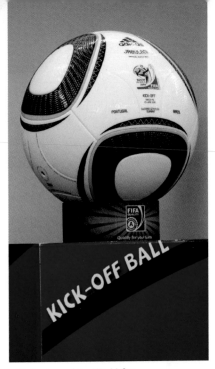

Blow football. Jabulani and the Vuvuzela – two of the unlikely stars of the World Cup.

Banging the drum for Joga Bonito...

...but Robben has the last laugh when things turn ugly in Port Elizabeth

Let's be having you! Ghana's answer to Delia Smith stirs up the crowd in Soccer City

Send in the clowns: Uruguayan fans – the pantomime villains – brave the Fanfest in Cape Town

Kiss of death: Even with two watches Diego can't see that it's time to let go of his beloved shirt

Brilliant orange. Not for the first time, the Dutch colonise Cape Town

Spain to win? The writing was on the ball

Ghosting out of the shadows onto centre stage Andrés Iniesta, *El Anti-Galáctico*

Sharing the pot of gold – the real challenge for World Cup 2010

the 1830s, Cape Town's then British rulers offered some the chance to buy their freedom. But this was only available for Muslims, the group perceived to offer the best chance of bringing new skills and wealth into a nascent economy. The seeds of a segregated society were being sown.

We drove up Long Street, through Cape Town's tightly packed commercial and administrative centre, and parked at the foot of Signal Hill. Soon the skyline opened up as we reached a residential area where rows of Dutch gabled houses in brilliant colours gleamed in the sunshine. We had arrived in Bo-Kaap, a settling point for the Cape Malay population after they had prised off their bonds during the emancipation programme. Colleen pointed to some red and yellow bunting draped between the houses, a remnant of the New Year celebrations when the coons marched through the streets. My politically correct buttocks clenched – the "what" marched? Colleen explained that "the coons" (a shortening of racoons) were the traditional minstrels, parading through town in their band colours to mark festive occasions. When Apartheid laws forbade public gatherings of more than four people, they made an exception for New Year's Day. A year's worth of celebration was poured into a 24-hour period.

I wandered up the hill, the blinding early morning sun picking out the rich, fresh colours of the houses: mint green, yolk yellow, duck-egg blue, rose pink. It felt like walking through a childhood dream: gingerbread houses, Toyland; what's the story in Balamory?

We made our way up Constitution Hill and parked outside a small general store. Shortly after Colleen had emerged with a brown paper bag, the reassuring smell of warm sugary dough filled the car. We had coffee in the District 6 Museum and Colleen fished the pastries out of the bag. I had tried these before in their Afrikaans guise, koek sisters – gluey sausages of deep fried syrup: sickly sweet – eat one and you are wired for the day, eat two and the hallucinations kick in. By contrast these warm, soft little torpedoes of delicately-sugared, artfully-spiced dough were a far more subtle delight. Colleen explained how every Sunday morning her street in District 6 awoke to the smell of fresh baking as neighbours did the rounds with brimming baskets. This was how the community operated: egalitarian, comfortable with itself, at ease with each other. You had doctors next door to fishermen, next door to lawyers, next door to gangsters. A richly diverse group rubbing along together, fusing cultures, sharing the space and their lives.

Walking around the museum, the black and white photographs on the wall poured with colour. Inevitably I was drawn to the sports pictures: irresistible line-ups of cricketers in flannels and blazers, neat moustaches and slicked-down hair, louchely dangling cigarettes; then the footballers with chests puffed out in their lace-up shirts, beaming with pride, bearing up a ribbon-strewn cup. For me the photograph that seemed to capture the spirit of the place was a chaotic mid-town scene, in which people spilled in and out of doorways and into the street, where vendors hawked and bustled, children chased and played, overhangs and balconies bore neighbours shouting to each other over washing lines. The cast were dressed to kill: spats and turbans, trilbies and curlers. Nosing through the midst of this seething mass of humanity, a double-decker London bus.

District 6 was a bulging treasure chest of life in which differences over class, race, religion or sexual orientation counted for nothing. The government hated it. Here was a mirror held up before the values of Apartheid reflecting its ugliest features, outing its underlying irrelevance. In the late sixties the Group Areas Act was invoked and the bulldozers rumbled in. The inhabitants of District 6 were scattered, relocated to new settlements far out of town – families were split, friendships severed, bands of musicians and teams of sportsmen were dragged apart. At one end of the museum's main hall the old street signs have been built into a tower reaching for the sky. Shortly after it opened one of the bulldozer drivers walked in and deposited them; they had been buried in his garden, and no doubt his conscience, for over twenty years.

As we headed out of town along the N2 the cooling towers at Athlone soon loomed into view. We left the highway and headed into the settlement of Langa. Pointing to new blocks of flats, Colleen explained that this area – 'the N2 Gateway' – had been targeted as a regeneration hotspot when it seemed that Athlone would have a prominent role to play in Cape Town's 2010 plans. The Gateway project has caused resentment within communities exiled to the Flats decades ago, perceiving preferential treatment for more recent arrivals.

In 2008 this tension between the various dispossessed groups thrown together on the increasingly overcrowded Flats erupted, responding to a wave of xenophobic violence sweeping down from the north targeting immigrants, notably the increasingly large numbers of Zimbabweans entering South Africa. The sight of bodies burning in the streets – a horrific throwback to the retribution reserved for informants during the State of Emergency – fuelled the lobby arguing that the country was slipping into lawless disarray. Not for the first time Sepp Blatter was forced to issue a public reaffirmation of his support for Fifa's 2010 'plan A'. Down at street level, football took some more pragmatic steps: the One Man Can project organised street tournaments in the Cape townships, aiming to heal the rifts between the different communities, and leading players spoke out to condemn the violence.

As we drove into Mitchell's Plain the streets began to close in around us as shacks and commerce gathered on all sides. Whole sheep heads – 'smilies' – beamed from hooks on the butcher's stall; next to them the local sangoma 'Mr Major' was in business in the dark, cool interior of a rusting shipping container. Despite the heat, young men walked around in flat caps and overcoats; an outward sign of their post-circumcision journey into manhood. We passed a ragged football pitch, trapped at the intersection of three roads which Colleen identified as a notorious car-jacking black-spot. A Saturday morning game was in progress, two sides in bright kit going at it as groups of young men gathered on the bonnets of BMWs to watch. A large rectangular amplifier behind one of the goals boomed out a relentless beat. The wind – which can howl through Cape Town – swept up litter which plastered the chicken wire fence running around the pitch. Every few minutes the blank expression of a 747 loomed behind play, skimming the fence, escaping the nearby airport.

We carried on into Gugulethu along Mew Way, joining a rally of vintage Japanese cars – Toyota Cressidas, Datsun Sunnys, Nissan Bluebirds – I had last seen screeching through the American cop shows of my youth. As the skyline opened up, the enormity of the township hit home: a low-lying endless sprawl. The only elevations rising from the clustered shacks were wooden electricity poles being slowly strangled by spidery wires leeching juice away into the labyrinth and the towering stalks of the street lights – sleek and futuristic, peering down at the primitive mess below. The further we travelled the thicker the air became; the sanitation services were under as much pressure as the electricity grid.

Eventually we arrived in Khayelitsha. The shacks stretched for miles. We had reached the outer limit of the Flats, a moveable boundary shifting monthly with every wave of new arrivals. Colleen explained that many people travelled down from the Eastern Cape, looking for work and broader horizons in the city. I wondered how many of them packed into these warrens still had dreams of the wide, lush beauty of the Transkei. Corrugated iron walls rattled and tarpaulin roofs flapped as gusty winds swept in from the ocean, swirling across the sand and rugged bushes. In the distance the highway roared; along its edge, in silhouette, a few young girls in their best, shortest dresses and high heels tottered towards slowing cars. The fresh sheet metal on the newest shacks shimmered under the burning sun, dimpled and silvery. Wandering through Bo-Kaap an hour earlier the bright sun had lit up the soft pastel colours of a dream; now it picked out the sharp metallic edges of a dazzling, nightmarish existence. We had reached the end of the food chain.

The following day I headed back to Athlone with my brother-in-law Cameron to watch Ajax Cape Town play a CAF Champions League match. The stadium was unrecognisable from my last visit. Gone were the rusting iron stands and crumbling brickwork; in their place twin grandstands with sleek steel girders arced through the sky. It resembled the kind of ground an ambitious Championship club would build to host their Premiership dreams and a selfish nostalgia washed over me as I recalled the rustic charm of the previous venue.

Cameron's memories of the old Athlone Stadium were somewhat different to my own. During the mid-eighties when he was heavily involved in student politics at UCT, the stadium had been a focal point for meetings and rallies. He recalled addressing a demonstration calling for Mandela's release, from a makeshift stage made from empty oil drums. The police fired teargas in an attempt to disperse the crowd and arrest the leadership, creating a foggy chaos full of screams and flailing batons. For Cameron these became familiar flashpoints as he dug himself deeper into the underground movement building the foundations from which the ANC could offer a realistic level of opposition to the Apartheid government. Elected as one of the few white ANC MPs in 1994, Cameron went on to become the minister for education and sport in the Western Cape. I asked him what he hoped for from 2010.

"The challenge is to take the game out of the stadium and into the communities, get people involved. The World Cup is not just about football, it should be a carnival; we want Cape Town to have fun, get caught up in the atmosphere. For me, it's about the fan parks with big screens, the visits from star players – imagine Beckham and Ronaldo pitching up in Gugs for a kickabout. The players will get a bigger picture of South African life and the kids in the township would never forget seeing these guys on their own doorstep.

"Our entrepreneurs from the townships must position themselves to build and strengthen businesses which grow beyond 2010 and create the jobs we so desperately need. We have to build more than new stadia, hotels and airport extensions; somehow this event has got to build foundations for new sports development programmes that will still be going strong in years to come. I hope that young people will be inspired by this event and realise that they can aspire to be the best in the world and that they should not stand back for anyone."

Despite the box-fresh feel of the venue, the atmosphere had familiar overtones from that long evening in the old stadium. It was Easter Sunday and there was a relaxed, holiday feel. The mix was the most cosmopolitan I had seen in any ground; there was even a knot of white students below us, honking their vuvuzelas. A queue of excited young boys, shouting, nudging and shoving each other, lined up for their chance to crank up a huge red and white air raid siren. The predominant social grouping was one that even the pettiness of Apartheid's multi-tiered racial classification system would struggle to pin down: Rastafarians. All around us dreadlocks dangled and swung; thick smoke billowed. The kids would calm down soon enough.

The low-key atmosphere was well-suited to the fixture. Ajax faced an afternoon stroll against a club several links below them in the football food chain: Anse Reunion FC. On the face of it the champion football team in the Seychelles shares a podium with Germany's funniest stand-up and the finest ice-skater in the Congo. But the mantle of favourites seemed to sit uneasily with Ajax.

Their rangy young striker, Nathan Paulse, strolled then darted, shimmied then spun, beguiling a pair of centre-backs that were more Laurel and Hardy than Lawrenson and Hansen. Soon enough someone lost their patience, a clothes-line arm swung out and the Ajax striker tumbled to the turf. Now it was time for another comedy double act: Little and Large, the Ajax stretcher bearers. On they came, beanpole at the front, pocket rocket at the rear, rising and falling, loping ludicrously, like X-ray footage of a pantomime horse in full gallop. There were some nice touches during the match for the crowd to applaud but the game shot its bolt in the first five minutes: for sheer entertainment value nothing could beat the keystone medics.

Ajax needed a creative spark, something different, to break down the Seychellian wall. It arrived in the diminutive shape of their No15, Mkhanyiseli Siwahla. He first made his name in 2002, aged 15, as the youngest player ever to score in South African professional football. Two years later it looked as though he may take a giant leap up the food chain when Barcelona called him for a trial. Had he made it at the Nou Camp, Siwahla would have had the chance to appear alongside his idol Ronaldinho, but it was not to be. Now 21, he had arrived at the difficult second album stage of his career; the child prodigy needed to stand up with the men. Watching his slight boyish frame racing around the pitch the Brazilian that sprung to mind was Robinho: feinting, swerving; swift, deft touches, spins at high speed – terrorising and mesmerising back-pedalling defenders. Tsamayas, shibobos, peddaldas, easy oasys, lollipops – dancing feet, in anyone's language.

Despite his stature he played without fear. He knew that his team were far superior; more tellingly it was clear that he backed his own prodigious skills against all comers. Desperate to make an impression and kick on up the ladder, he tried everything and most of it came off.

A few weeks earlier up in Pretoria I had watched Chiefs take on Supersport United and seen a similar spark. Supersport's No20, Kermit Erasmus – a chunky figure with a tufty white mohican splitting a bullet-like head – terrorised the Amakhosi backline. The baying of the Chiefs fans around me seemed motivated more by envy than wrath; this was the kind of dash and verve they wanted from their own players. Every time Kermit skinned the full-back or ghosted away from tackles in a whirl of tsamayas, the Chiefs faithful showered him with curses as they tried to hide grins of admiration. Eventually his number came up as Chiefs' strapping left-back clattered in from behind, sending the striker crashing into the advertising boards. The crowd fell silent. A gaunt, ancient Chiefs fan in front of me rose slowly from his seat and raised his vuvuzela straight out before him, like a sangoma lining up a powerful curse.

"Eh, revvy, revvy – send that naughty boy home; he is too jealous, man."

The Chiefs fan next to me turned and smiled: "Eish, this guy Erasmus, he's like Rooney, hey?"

Watching Rooney's desperate display against the Algerians, I remembered this observation – how Wayne's global brand portrayed a fearless firebrand, an instinctive bull-at-a-gate player – *Inkabi* – and wondered what was going wrong. The 18-year-old that rampaged through Euro 2004 was not the same player that was spitting with frustration as he left the field at Green Point in 2010, boos ringing in his ears.

Conventional wisdom tells us that he had become a far better player – he'd lost the reckless streak, he was more controlled, he had acquired a better all-round understanding of the game. Which presumably means he had a clear appreciation of what is expected – demanded – when you are playing for England in a World Cup facing a team from way down the football food chain. All of which just might explain why, on that particular night, a player who had learnt his game on the backstreets, in the process developing an astonishing speed of thought and deftness of touch, couldn't trap a bag of wet cement.

Although footballers' achievements are usually contingent on what they do with their feet, head or hands, it is another body part that tends to define them as players. It has been suggested that Rooney's game relies on an innate sense of positioning and movement – a highly developed 'football brain'. Before the 2006 World Cup Professor Oliver Hoener, a German academic from the University of Mainz, refined this theory: "Mindlessness is a good quality for a striker and good decisions have nothing to do with intelligence, which is why players such as Wayne Rooney show so much genius on the pitch." Less conscious thought, more instinct – whichever way you look at it, it's all still happening upstairs. For the more romantic, a player's success or failure depends not on what he keeps between his ears, but on the large organ pulsing beneath the badge on his shirt. You often hear talk of a certain performer who has a 'big heart', or others who 'wear their heart on their sleeve'.

Watching the likes of Rooney, Siwahla and Erasmus at their best, much of course depends on speed of thought, but there is also a love for playing the game a certain way: with boundless ambition, without fear, with joy. And joy, one hopes, while manifesting itself as a cognitive response, is an emotion that owes as much to the heart as the head.

As for football in Cape Town once Rooney and the rest have headed home, it's an equally complicated story. The football-loving community is well established on the Cape Flats – clutching the hope offered by sport, fending off the despair of their surroundings – getting behind clubs like Santos, Cape Town Spurs and Seven Stars. When a European superpower swallowed the latter two it was a strange kind of progress. Money in, talent out. The 2010 World Cup promised to reassert some balance at a rejuvenated, regenerated Athlone Stadium – at the gateway to the Flats, but in sight of the city – at the heart of Cape Town football. But while the newly refurbished grounds bordering the townships in Athlone and Phillipi operated as practice venues for visiting teams, the main focus was on the more salubrious Green Point, leaving the Cape Town game spread far and wide. The future for the new stadium is unclear; the Stormers, the Western Cape's rugby force, may well move there from their current home across town at Newlands.

Santos will stay at Athlone; Ajax are moving further into the Flats to a new home at Phillipi.

If you do ever find yourself in Cape Town, once you have climbed Table Mountain, shopped at the Waterfront and walked the beautiful gardens at Kirstenbosch, take a stroll into Newlands Forest and seek out that view of the whole city. I can't decide whether it fills me with hope or despair. Before the World Cup, during a visit to Cape Town to check on progress with the new stadium, Sepp Blatter had no doubts: "Football will solve problems, and football will bring everyone together, in politics and in sports," he said. No offence Joe, but for a more realistic view, albeit from the foot of the scaffold, I'm with Sydney Carton.

"I see a beautiful city and a brilliant people rising from this abyss, and, in their struggles to be truly free, in their triumphs and defeats, through long years to come, I see the evil of this time and of the previous time of which this is the natural birth, gradually making expiation for itself and wearing out."

STATE OF THE UNION

DESPITE RELOCATING TO THE RACY ENVIRONS OF SOHO SQUARE, the English Football Association still retains the look and feel of a bastion of conservative stability. The jewel in their crown is the FA Cup, a competition they promote forcefully, even to the point of broadcasting the draw for each round of ties. These days, this is usually presided over by former players, grinning self-consciously and cracking the odd lame gag as they delve into a plastic tub and root around for numbered balls. But in years gone by the event had a whiff of ceremony, featuring a pair of septuagenarian FA officials in immaculate navy blazers solemnly withdrawing ivory balls from a blood-red, velvet purse, occasionally emitting a jowly 'harrumph' when the likes of Kettering Town were handed a trip to Old Trafford. When a sharp-eyed television executive realised that the old boys were doing nothing to attract the all-important yoof market they were shown the door, but the image endures. If someone put a gun to my head, handed me a pencil and paper and asked me to draw 'the FA' – an unlikely scenario, but we live in uncertain times – I suspect that my shaking hand would sketch a blazered old fart, peering down his nose at me whilst rummaging in a sack of rattling balls.

It therefore came as something of a surprise when, in 2004, this cornerstone of the establishment was plunged into a bonkbuster of a tabloid crisis. Standing calmly in the eye of the storm was the then England manager Sven-Göran Eriksson, a man recruited at great expense by the FA to deliver not just results, but a style of play immortalised by the Dutch legend Ruud Gullit as "shexshee football". A grey, bespectacled figure with a singular talent for saying nothing at great length – "Vell, I sink dat maybe we can play some nice football and, who knows, maybe ve can vin…I hope, but hey, you know dat is da game, heh, heh, and perhaps sometimes somesink vill happen dat you did not sink vould happen, yes?" – behind closed doors Eriksson was a throbbing, turbo-charged love piston, pumping away remorselessly at a harem of attractive, much younger women. If the players had emulated their coach's energy, drive and ability to score away from home, they could have given the Brazilians the hiding of their lives. Sadly, although Sven clearly had enough patter to melt the heart of a marble nun, he could never find the words to coax the best out of a talented group of England players – "Vell, I sink maybe try to kick dee boll into dee goll, yes?" – and the team, unlike the coach, never quite managed to go all the way.

The imbroglio in Soho Square involved Sven, the FA's then chief executive, his PA and a glut of tabloid headlines that jumbled the words "stunner", "romped", "married" and "shame". In any other country the media and public reaction may have been more restrained, perhaps even ambivalent, but here the story was celebrated as the best of British. A couple of middle-aged men in suits, with their trousers sagging around their ankles, eagerly pursuing a buxom young secretary round and round the desk – you could almost hear the Benny Hill theme parping away happily in the background.

By contrast the crises that have befallen South African football administrators over the years have tended to offer a little more substance. Take for example the long and tortuous journey to arrive at a fully functioning professional league.

During the 1970s, as the NPSL (the non-white league) flourished, with fanatical crowds flocking to see star players like Kaizer and Jomo, the white NFL suffered by comparison. A once vibrant competition contested by clubs like Durban City, Highlands Park and Hellenic had drawn crowds in excess of 30,000 to high-profile games. The logical approach would have been to integrate the best elements of the two, but this was Apartheid South Africa; logic be damned. Keen to avoid a mixed-race league, the Football Association of South Africa (FASA), who controlled access to most of the grounds, refused permission for the staging of any fixtures that matched teams from the two factions. Recognising the maxim 'adapt or perish', a handful of NFL clubs took matters into their own hands. Highlands Park added colour and talent to their squad in the shape of Jerry Sadike and Kenneth 'The Horse' Mokhoja, while Wits University took a side into Soweto to play a friendly against Chiefs, and were promptly arrested. Despite these efforts, by the end of the decade the NFL had disintegrated; most of the clubs disappeared without trace as the fans drifted away in the direction of rugby fields and TV screens broadcasting action from the English football league.

Despite its supremacy and popularity, the NPSL was not without its problems and in the mid-eighties a major power shift rocked its foundations. In 1985, looking to secure better terms, a breakaway group led by Kaizer Motaung formed their own National Soccer League – soon to be rechristened the Castle League, after South African Breweries stepped in with R400,000 of sponsorship. But it was not a clean break. Some officials and players stayed loyal to the old regime, and the inaugural fixture of the new league was marred by a shocking incident.

The match was a Johannesburg derby at Ellis Park, between Jomo Cosmos and Pirates. Shortly after the teams had emerged onto the pitch, a second 'alternative' Pirates XI were led out by their coach China Hlongwane. Enraged by this humiliating show of disunity, a dozen Pirates fans leapt from the crowd and attacked Hlongwane with knives. He suffered 55 stab wounds, all captured by the attendant television cameras. One eye-witness recalled: "Hlongwane fought back like an angry, frustrated bull in a Spanish festival, unable to gore a single one of the 'matadors' who stabbed him and then darted out of harm's way."

Contrast the Hlongwane incident with the Eriksson affair. A proud man standing up for his beliefs cut down by an angry knife-wielding mob, versus a spot of how's-your-father over the filing cabinet. A model of cultural diversity: *Titus Andronicus* squares up to *Carry On Bonking*.

AT THE CONCLUSION OF THE SECOND ROUND OF GROUP GAMES the English FA and SAFA were as one, united in the face of a common dilemma. Their teams teetered on the brink, facing an early expulsion from the World Cup and the commercial, political and social implications that came with it. Reports suggested that the FA and Capello would part company if England failed to progress, continuing an unfortunate trend. The spring of 2010 saw the demise of the FA's chief executive Ian Watmore, its chair Lord Triesman, and the team captain, John Terry – the last two embroiled in variations of the tabloid bonkbuster. Terry's removal was the result of swift, decisive action by Capello; the return match was a messier affair.

The manager had agreed to let the players have a beer – giusto il uno, per favore! – as they soaked up the Algerian result. It is said that John Terry felt the mood was ripe for revolution, time for the players to confront the manager over his rigid selection policies and processes. At his next press conference Terry hinted that a showdown was imminent. It never happened and Capello publicly chided his player for speaking out of turn: "This is the big mistake – a very big mistake. It's not revolution. It's the mistake of another player – no more…The mistake is that you have to speak with the players, with me, with the dressing room."

The bleated propaganda from the phoney war in Rustenburg was soon drowned out by a series of atomic booms from the picturesque Garden Route town of Knysna. Nicolas Anelka lit the fuse, launching a volley of abuse at his coach Raymond Domenech and was soon heading home. The players were revolting – maybe they wouldn't even show up for the last game. There was no room for tabloidese in *Le Figaro*'s artful dissection: "It is collective suicide," it said, "... the French team has heaped ridicule on itself in front of the whole world. It was almost hallucinatory. This is a psychodrama that will go down in the history of the World Cup. The French team has been reduced to ashes." A sad end for a team that had performed wonders in 1998, unifying a rugby-mad nation behind a football team built upon the talents of a multi-cultural squad.

As he prepared his troops for their last hurrah, Carlos Alberto Parreira was also looking for a landmark performance: "History will talk about this game." Of course, this being South Africa, history already has plenty to say for itself, not least where football is concerned.

Travelling the country before the tournament, talking to a wide variety of people about the game, I was struck by how often opinion seemed to cluster at the extremes. The prevailing view amongst whites tended to be dismissive: it's all about tricks and showing off, a fanatical devotion to a mediocre sport; Bafana Bafana will never emulate the success of the national rugby and cricket teams, etc, etc. The black fans that I sat alongside in various grounds around the country were indeed hopelessly devoted to their clubs, feasting off crumbs of skill or excitement – wallowing in defeat, unrealistic about future success – pretty much like football fans all over the world.

A few days after returning from Mpumalanga I was sitting in traffic on Jan Smuts Drive, heading for the offices of the PSL and a conversation with Ronnie Schloss, chief operating officer of the PSL, a man better qualified than most to provide some insights into the divisions within South African football culture.

Ronnie's life in football had begun with Wits University and, after injury curtailed his playing career, continued in administration when he took on the role of club president. He had recognised before most that the NFL could not compete with the more vibrant and popular NPSL, and made strenuous attempts to support the integration of the two leagues. Ronnie was amongst those arrested by the army in Soweto (along with his six- and eight-year-old children) for taking his Wits side into the township for the friendly match with Chiefs. His subsequent roles in shaping the post-Apartheid landscape of South African football have included a guiding hand on the 2006 and 2010 World Cup bids. His take on World Cup 2010 was uncomplicated:

"It will be an African experience, with its own peculiarities and problems. It will be different, interesting. Above all, the ordinary man or woman in the street will ask how 2010 has improved their life. Soccer must be able to answer that question if the tournament is to be truly considered a success."

As someone who laboured to integrate the racially divided leagues I was interested in Ronnie's views on the apparent divisions within the South African football audience. He explained that, at its peak, the white NFL attracted a huge following but its sudden demise left few traces. In the 1980s black teams dominated, playing games at venues bordering townships such as Soweto, Athlone and Umlazi. The growing sense of tension as the country descended into a State of Emergency provided little incentive for white fans to travel to games. With the added distractions of cricket, rugby and an emerging world of televised sports, white football fans, indeed white football, seemed to disappear, almost overnight.

I drove away from the PSL offices deep in thought. It seemed bizarre that a whole population of football fans could disappear in the blink of an eye. I could understand the factors mitigating the original exodus of white fans. After all, most of their clubs folded after failing to hop aboard the runaway NPSL bandwagon. Switching their affections to, say, Chiefs or Pirates would have taken them into parts of town that the law – and perhaps common sense – deemed to be off limits at that time. The sad thing is that even after the fall of Apartheid, and the changes that followed, it seems that few white fans have come back for another go.

This sense of detachment struck me powerfully one Sunday afternoon at the King Zwelithini Stadium, near the Umlazi township on the outskirts of Durban. I had paid my money and settled down on the concrete steps under the shade of the solitary stand. As kick-off time approached and the fans trickled in I was soon surrounded by a happy, noisy, expectant crowd. Well, almost surrounded. Until some latecomers arrived, the area around me remained noticeably vacant. There was no hostility or antipathy, just a vague sense of awkwardness. An eye-level photograph of the stand would have shown a near capacity crowd and in its midst me, sitting on an island of space in a sea of humanity, like the star of a desperately unimaginative advertising campaign for deodorant. What's wrong with this picture? In South Africa they have a word for it: in English 'separateness', in Afrikaans 'apartheid'. Please don't misunderstand me. I am not suggesting that white fans are in any way *precluded* from attending matches, just that, for whatever reason, the same sports-mad people that happily hoover up cricket and rugby are not being sucked in by football.

I was so deep in thought that I had absolutely no idea where I was going. The road network linking the various suburbs of Johannesburg is a complex of threads knotted together with intersections stringing out on to various highways out of town. I had followed a straightforward route to the PSL on a single page of my street map. Now, distracted, I had drifted off course and was heading for a spaghetti junction of flyovers to destinations that neither looked nor sounded even vaguely familiar. Eventually I spied salvation in the shape of a sign to Gold Reef City.

Although it sounds like the kind of mythical destination a Victorian explorer called Sir 'Corky' Scrotlington-Farquar would devote their life to finding, Gold Reef City is in fact an "historical amusement park" based around a mining theme. A few years earlier, with time to kill before our flight home, my wife and I had frittered away a couple of hours there, eating prospector steaks with golden fries and riding a rickety, faux mineshaft train that dragged its screaming cargo through the air in a series of corkscrew loops and plunges. It was certainly amusing but quite how historically accurate, I couldn't say. As we emerged from the park I had spotted the Apartheid Museum across the road and heard the words 'next time' drift rather sheepishly into my head. The time had come.

To enter the museum one must first pass through one of the turnstiles, marked 'whites' and 'non-whites', according to the colour of your admission pass, leading on through a pair of parallel, caged walkways. The point of exit from these cages is not immediately apparent, by design, and for a few brief moments both myself and the visitors passing on the other side of the fence exchanged confused, slightly panicky glances. It's a neat, subtle way of preparing you for what is to follow.

Inside the main complex the museum follows a chronological description of its subject, leading you step by step through its rise and eventual fall. Early on visitors are presented with a wall of laws – white lettering cut on to a black marble tablet – recording the legislative history of Apartheid. Although the ideology really only acquired its name when a coalition of two Nationalist Afrikaans parties swept to power in 1948, racially discriminatory laws were already well established in South Africa. Decades earlier the British colonial regime had regulated the freedoms of non-white South Africans by restricting rights to vote, own land and move freely. The raft of laws introduced by the National Party, following their election, took this underlying principle of subjugation through supremacy and made a science of it. The fastidious detail of the measures enacted during the first five years of the new administration reveals a desire not simply to exert control over people, but to classify, compartmentalise and confine them.

The Population Registration Act (1950) required each citizen to register according to their racial group – black, white or coloured – and carry an ID card. Here the notorious 'pencil test' was deployed: if it fell through your hair, life would be easier. Once you had been classified, every aspect of life became regulated: where you lived (Groups Areas Act), where you sat on the bus or beach (Reservation of Separate Amenities Act), who you could marry (Prohibition of Mixed Marriages Act) or even date (Immorality Act). In 1952 the ultimate symbol of control arrived in the shape of the Pass Laws, requiring every black South African over the age of 18 to carry a pass book detailing where they were going and with whose authority.

A window cut into the wall of laws looked into a darkened room in which dozens of nooses hung limply from the ceiling. A series of passages then led through a maze of cages, the walls of which followed the ruinous impact of this legal wrecking ball. Flickering newsreel footage showed Prime Minster Hendrik Verwoerd – one of the chief architects of Apartheid – delivering a series of hearty pronouncements of its merits and necessity. Elsewhere on the cage sombre faces peered out from enlarged reproductions of ID cards and passes, alongside their classification and travel permissions. Other videos showed the first signs of unrest – uprisings met with uncompromising police responses – and footage of an assassination attempt on Verwoerd.

The cages were dimly lit and as I walked down the passage the soundtrack from the video newsreels merged into a confusion of shouted Afrikaans political rhetoric, gunshots, screams, wails and angry cries. The sad faces gazing out of the gloom added to a chilling, sobering experience.

Further on, the photographs and videos revealed the liberal use of the Suppression of Communism Act and Terrorism Act, to empower the government to round up and imprison dissidents. Here the documentation of the Defiance Campaign reached its first significant peak, with a series of stills and films showing the rise of the armed wing of the ANC, *Umkhonto we Sizwe* (Spear of the Nation), under the guidance of their charismatic leader. I would guess that, for most people of my generation, our first sight of Nelson Mandela was of the grey-haired elder statesman, emerging back into the world at the turn of the nineties, measured in tone and poise. But here in these still and moving images I could see the brawny shoulders, honed by sessions in the boxing gym, of the loquacious, forcefully persuasive young lawyer.

You can try to describe the iniquities of a society in a library of words but a handful of photographs will tell a thousand stories. I was fortunate that my visit to the museum coincided with an exhibition of pictures from Ernest Cole's book *House of Bondage*, revealing scenes of everyday life from an oppressed, disenfranchised community. The trains with bodies literally hanging off, arriving in the city for work; a queue of miners lining up to have food slopped onto their tin plates with a long-handled shovel; the classroom full of children squatting, packed like sardines, beads of sweat running down their faces as they scratched with chalk on slates. The image that stopped me short showed a young girl with a single tear rolling down her cheek, cradling a crying baby; the caption read: "Photo of Gracie Matjila, her baby sister was hungry and it reminded her that she was too." The final picture in the series showed a blonde, white baby bouncing along a tree-lined avenue in the city, swaddled snugly on the back of his black nanny.

Turning the corner I found myself looking back into the room full of nooses. This side of the wall featured a roll-call of those executed for political reasons. The name Steve Biko stood out. A student leader and founder of the Black Consciousness Movement, Biko was a razor-sharp thorn in the flesh of the Nationalist government. The BCM was heavily involved in the organisation of the Soweto uprising of 1976, a march by students against the predominance of Afrikaans in the classroom that ultimately escalated into a bloody riot. The police met stones with bullets and in the ensuing chaos hundreds were killed. Another picture that speaks volumes about this period of South African history is a famous photograph taken by Sam Nzima showing a man running from the chaos, carrying the fatally-wounded body of 12-year-old Hector Pieterson.

The link between the BCM and the Soweto riots convinced the government that the time had come to silence Biko. A year after the uprising he was arrested under the Terrorism Act. A few months later he was dead. At the time the police claimed that an extended hunger strike and suicide attempts were responsible. Subsequent investigations and admissions made to the Truth and Reconciliation Commission revealed that Biko suffered a major head trauma whilst in custody, was chained to a window grill for 24 hours and then stripped naked and driven in the back of a truck over 1,500 kilometres to Pretoria to finally receive the medical treatment he was long past needing.

Behind the noose room a typical solitary confinement cell had been recreated. It was about 6ft x 3ft, battleship grey, with a single, narrow slit pouring light in from above. Detainees could be held in cells like this for three, 100-day spells. A smooth, blood-red wall curving away from the cell carried more video screens showing images from the 1976 uprising and its aftermath. At the end of the wall a Casspir was parked, and I had a sudden jolt of recognition; we were now entering the period in Apartheid history that I remembered. Watching the video footage of the Casspir – a bellicose, armoured police vehicle swathed in grilles – in action, rumbling into townships, dispersing crowds, dispensing 'justice', I saw the images that had defined South Africa for me as a child of the late 1970s and early 80s.

TV news reports in jarring, vivid colour showing ugly clashes between crowds of black people – dancing and chanting as they marched, fists pumping the air – and the white security forces sitting atop tanks, brandishing rifles. I recalled hearing confusing new words like 'sanctions', 'boycott' and 'apartheid' and that I had made little sense of any of it. The only solid conclusion I had drawn was that South Africa was a colourful, sunny place full of anger, conflict, suffering and sadness, a million miles away from the suburban street on which I practised keepy-uppy and tried unsuccessfully to perform 'endoes' on my Raleigh Burner. I climbed into the back of the Casspir and peered out through the mesh-covered slit windows, trying to imagine how it might feel to be rumbling towards an angry mob. Within the dark, musty cabin there was a stale reek which I took to be the smell of fear.

The museum's final corridors brought me to the turn of the nineties and the frantic negotiations surrounding Mandela's release. Looking at the video footage in this section the simple hypothesis from my childhood – nasty white men shooting at nice black men – starts to look flawed. With the country edging towards an inevitable power shift, one sees the emergence of a bloody, tribal conflict between militant factions of the ANC and the Inkatha Freedom Party. Energised by the spectre of bloodthirsty gangs marauding through the land, we also see Eugène Terre'Blanche bashing a lectern, talking a good fight.

LISTENING TO PARREIRA TALK A GOOD MATCH PRIOR TO HIS last group game, I doubt many people really believed that Bafana Bafana could rise from the canvas, catch France with a sucker punch and sneak into the knockout stages. But it so nearly worked out that way. For a glorious period in the first half The Boys were all over the former World and European Champions. I loved the reaction of Katlego Mphela when he scrambled home the second goal. No lavish celebrations, he just plunged into the goal, grabbed the ball, jammed it under his armpit and headed back to the centre circle – a man on a mission. Mphela had further chances: there was the curling shot against the crossbar and then, driving into the penalty area, an ankle tap from behind knocked him off balance at the crucial moment. He stayed upright – trying to stagger onward when many might have flung themselves to the floor – typifying an honest performance from a team fighting stacked odds. By contrast the French, now heavily type-cast as the villains of the piece, limped out in shame – Domenech's steadfast refusal to shake Parreira's hand at the final whistle providing the final, tawdry tableau.

It is somewhat ironic that the setting for Bafana Bafana's last stand was the Free State Stadium in Bloemfontein – a rugby ground in a city which still feels like the white heart of South Africa, capital of what was until relatively recently the 'Orange' Free State. It was here in the early 19th century that a community of Dutch farmers settled after trekking north from the Cape in search of better grazing lands. Having established themselves at the centre of a country of such racial, cultural and linguistic diversity, 'the Boers' established their own Republic of the Oranje-Vrystaat and language, Afrikaans. When offered the warm embrace of British colonialism in the latter years of the century they defended their independence vigorously. This keen sense of identity and nationalism is reflected to this day in the perception of the Free State as a bedrock of conservative values, at times struggling to cope with South Africa's evolving society.

Unsurprisingly, the region's sporting idols tend to be drawn from the world of cricket and rugby: Allan 'Wit Blitz' (white lightning) Donald terrorised the world's batsmen during the nineties and the monstrous Os du Randt propped up a World Cup-winning front row. But the city is also home to Bloemfontein Celtic: a club founded in 1969 as Mangaung United, only to be rechristened in the mid-eighties in honour of the Glasgow club. Their fans, the *Siwelele,* are widely regarded as the best in the country. The high profile of the Gauteng clubs tends to secure a level of devotion to Chiefs and Pirates amongst floating voters nationwide; it's curious but heartening to find a fervent group following a mid-table club stuck out in a traditional rugby outpost like the Free

State. Before the World Cup began I spent a memorable afternoon watching Celtic trying to rescue their season. The first challenge was finding the legendary Seisa Ramabodu Stadium.

The pictures I had seen of Bloemfontein were of handsome old court houses and churches, set amongst well-tended gardens full of the city's signature white roses. I expected grandeur and fountains of blooms. What I got, walking into the central district, was a pair of gut-wrenchingly ugly, biscuit-coloured tower blocks topped with grimy-looking observation chambers. In their day they were no doubt seen as futuristic, edgy designs; now tired, dirty and faintly sinister, they looked like the backdrop to a director's cut of *Blade Runner* re-shot in Darlington. I crossed Nelson Mandela Drive and walked into a large park. In its centre a man-made lake – Loch Logan – was bordered by a large, sprawling shopping mall. Halfway across the park I saw floodlights rising and assumed I was in luck, but this was the Free State Stadium, a large muscular bowl serving up rugby to fans of the local Super 14 side, The Cheetahs.

With dirty clouds gathering I sought shelter in an old shopping arcade off George Street. The shops catered for the budget end of the market; outside the street vendors undercut them. Meat was their main commodity – scrawny, roughly-plucked chickens were piled in crates, hunks of pink and bloody flesh dangled from hooks. The traders sold with gusto, booming out patter through crackly PA systems, rolling their 'r's over the thumping beat of the nearby taxi rank. The sky had all but fallen in at this point. It was a familiar scene of despair shrugged off with spirit.

The contrast between the gleaming retail experience over at Loch Logan and this earthy, forgotten corner was stark. Wherever you walked in the mall the swish of mops followed hot on your heels. In the old town square it was hard to tell where the litter ended and the ground began. It is convenient that the Free State Stadium sits close by the new waterfront complex. Visitors for 2010 could be bussed in, catch the game, nip into the mall for an overpriced Bafana shirt, suck up a swift cappuccino on the boardwalk and get the hell out without ever catching sight of the real heart of the town.

Looking at the 2010 venues one senses a certain reluctance to site anything too close to the harsher realities of daily life. Cape Town is the prime example, where the decision to erect a new stadium in Green Point – an affluent coastal suburb far away from the football heartlands of the Cape Flats – baffled and irritated both communities. Thirty-odd kilometres separate the new Moses Mabhida complex on Durban's waterfront from the happy chaos of the King Zwelithini Stadium, but it feels like a million miles.

Eventually I spotted some shirts with green and white hoops and joined them in a sweaty crush in the back of a minibus taxi. The man upon whose lap I was all but sitting introduced himself as Simphiwe. He was wearing an old Liverpool shirt and as we fell into conversation about the Spanish revolution at Anfield, a certain irony struck me. As an English football fan I could be reviled, an export from the home of the hooligan, but in Bloem, I suspect I was more welcome than a white local. I told him about my experiences at football matches and how I could not understand why more white people were not interested in the game.

"It's a shame, when you have things like this," Simphiwe explained. "You see how people fall back into the old ways; black and white, them and us. There are guys, young guys, who look back to a past they never even knew. They see the ANC and the corruption stories, and they look at Zim and get all worked up. But this is a minority element – it just gets all the press. With Celtic you will see some real fans; these guys keep the club next to their heart."

At the stadium we settled down on the concrete steps and were soon surrounded by noise and life – friends assembled, greetings and insults whistled back and forth. An ancient gent, a toothless grin splitting his rumpled face as he peered out from beneath the brim of a brown bowler hat, fussed around his antique clique; wagging fingers, bellowing accusations, cuffing ears. Suddenly he grabbed the ankles of the baby of the group – a tubby eightysomething – holding his legs out straight, goading him into attempting escape: "Eh? Eh? Eh?..." These boys were old hands; they had brought squares of foam to cushion their weary buttocks against the remorseless concrete steps.

To my right the Bishop Stand – Seisa Ramabodu's answer to the Kop – was still largely unpopulated. Directly across from where I was sitting a tunnel provided an entrance into the ground, and a few fans were drifting in. The match kicked off, exploding into a breakneck opening ten minutes. I could not understand why the supposedly best fans in the league were not around to see this. And then I heard it. A low rumble of melodic song drifting towards the ground from the roads leading up to the stadium. Rich, choral chants, punctuated by claps and the orchestrated honk of countless vuvuzelas. In the distance I could see a slow procession wending its way towards the ground, collecting strays from the surroundings streets. Through the tunnel and along the touchline they marched; an army come to battle under their banners, clarions calling their arrival. I could see why opposing teams revered these fans. Individually the elements were familiar: horns, sirens, flags, singing, dancing, but there was an organisation, a togetherness. Celtic won a corner and a thousand vuvuzelas swung to the heavens to proclaim it, like a forest of spears raised before the charge.

Celtic scored. The deep concrete beneath me shook. A bullet header from the edge of the area was heading for the keeper's embrace, before a second forehead diverted it into the roof of the net. A few minutes later the Celtic keeper stooped to collect a gentle shot only to see it nip between his ankles and trickle over the goal-line. It was the kind of slapstick moment that tends to find its way onto DVDs, often accompanied by the jaunty toot of a swanee whistle. The crowd groaned, the half-time whistle blew.

The PA system belted out some mindless Europop and a dozen teenage girls ran out on to the pitch. They wore Celtic kit modified for titillation – a tight shirt tied above the midriff, buttock-skimming shorts, knee-high socks – and carried pom poms. One of the old crew in front of me emitted a guttural growl of approval, like Sid James in *Carry on Cleo* watching Amanda Barrie frolicking in a bath of ass's milk.

The second half got underway and the crowd upped their game. A new round of singing began led by a male lead calling the masses to respond. The soloist had a beautiful plaintiff edge to his voice, nailing the difficult high notes, holding them in the grip of a rich incantation. The group response was just as lovely; deeply melodic, almost mournful. I have never heard anything quite like it.

A few drops of rain began to fall and the gloom seemed to seep into the players, as the game looked set to drift towards a stalemate. And then Black Leopards scored. It came from nowhere: a speculative boot up the field from the edge of the visitors' penalty box became an incisive through-ball once it had skidded off the crown of a Celtic centre-back. The Leopards left-wing swooped and slotted the ball past the stranded keeper.

The steady murmur of discontent that had been rumbling around the stand now bubbled up as a frothing explosion of rage. It was bad enough to be held to a draw by the league's bottom team, but defeat? Too much. The Bishop Stand became the epicentre of the building quake. Amidst the howls of outrage and angry, accusatory finger-jabbing, a white, polystyrene take-away box fluttered from the top of the stand, twirling gently to earth like a winged sycamore seed. More litter followed, then plastic bottles, then glass bottles; a couple of vuvuzelas thumped off the turf like blunt javelins. Fans began to gather against the fencing separating them from the pitch. A knot of tension tightened in my stomach as I recalled why such fences had been pulled down in British grounds two decades earlier. The shower of litter became a downpour. A few bodies were now scaling the fence. Stewards rushed hurriedly to the scene.

And then Celtic scored. Like most in the ground I had all but forgotten the players. From the corner of my eye I had seen them gather in the Leopards goalmouth for a corner. The ball curled in, the keeper aimed a terrific haymaker at it, missed, and a defender headed it off the line down into the box where it was subjected to a wild bout of penalty-area pinball. Like a bar of soap escaping a clenched fist, the ball suddenly popped up above the mêlée. It fell into a confusion of whirling limbs that somehow propelled it into the roof of the net. Now there are bicycle kicks and there are bicycle kicks. During his pomp at Juve, leading the line with a shaven, bullet-shaped head, Gianluca Vialli turned this art into a science. Rotating through the air like a diver – a tightly packed ball of muscular motion – Luca's overhead special was a neat, compact manoeuvre. In bicycling terms he brought to mind a racer bombing into the final straight. Aesthetically speaking, the effort that earned Celtic a point that afternoon was more like a drunken, penniless rickshaw driver steering his livelihood over a cliff in a final act of desperation.

It took a little while for the crowd to register what was going on. Anger turned to joy, but it was short-lived. Stealing a point at the death from a weak team was not what these fans had turned out to see. Celtic had enjoyed a bright start to the season, nosing around the upper reaches of the table; this result confirmed their decline and fall.

The stand around me began to empty as fans headed for home, muttering and grumbling. The oldest man in Africa snatched up his foam square, grimaced toothlessly, tugged the brim of his bowler over his eyes, clipped one of his crew round the ear and shuffled away up the steps. Over in the Bishop Stand the ugly mood returned. The flurries of litter and bottles resumed, the fence rattled under the weight of climbers. A group of small boys swarmed into the grandstand and dashed up the steps, heading for the deserted corporate boxes. They hopped into the boxes, grabbing at leftover food and swigging down the dregs of abandoned drinks, chucking the empties over the side. Soon the steps around me were covered, ringing to the jarring sound of shattering glass and rolling tin cans.

A number of fans had cleared the fence and were advancing towards the stewards protecting the pitch. A strapping matron joined them and I wondered if she would urge calm. She picked up a bottle and led the charge. I gave Simphiwe a quizzical look. He shrugged and turned to fight his way up the steps through the chaos of glass and litter.

"He always dresses like that. I don't know why. Go safe."

I squinted back towards the leader of the mob. Beneath a straggling green wig I could now see a beard clinging to a set of chins. The vast green bra worn over the shirt was an esoteric sartorial touch that my initial glance had missed. I could not tell you what he had stuffed it with, only that he had plenty of it.

The thing that struck me most about the *Siwelele* was their unity. They marched to the stadium as one, the beautiful singing was harmonised perfection; even the vuvuzelas – normally a jumbled traffic-jam soundtrack of honks and parps – seemed to meld together into a collective hum. And when the team let them down they had a little riot and then headed for home together – an endless green and white striped snake, winding its way back into the townships around the Seisa Ramabodu.

Bafana Bafana drew on a similar unity in Bloemfontein, singing their way down the tunnel and then forming into a tight huddle before launching a concerted assault on the fatally divided French. The country celebrated victory over Les Bleus as they had in the lead-up to the opening ceremony – with a joyous riot of noise and colour. As hosts the South Africans were world class, as competitors they fell a little short. I hope that Bafana's spirited efforts draw a few converts to the round ball, but the challenge still looks daunting. The separation between the worlds of football and rugby, entrenched in the Apartheid days, is hard to shift; often it feels like a triumph of perception over reality. During the 2009 Confederations Cup some reporters noted with disdain how the Bafana fans booed their white defender Matt Booth – a 6ft 4in powerhouse, a useful line-out jumper in another life. In fact, they were praising, not booing: "Boooooooo-th!"

At the risk of stating the obvious, a sporting group harbouring any ambitions for long-term success needs unity – from the administrators, through the management and coaches, down to the players. When England took on Slovenia in Port Elizabeth there were signs that the disharmony of the preceding days had been cast aside. The defence, marshalled by Terry, were well organised and compact for 80 minutes and then, for the final ten, they morphed into a gangling red monster, sprouting feet, shins and foreheads to block the path of successive Slovenian surges. Pretty it was not, but what better way to bond the team than with a good old fashioned, eyes bulging, backs-to-the-wall, for God's sake hoof it anywhere, utterly desperate rearguard action. There was an urgently assembled huddle at the final whistle and then on came Capello, marching across the pitch to embrace the players – not the kind of visceral, weepy bear hugs you might get from José, but a nice round of heartily stiff slaps on the back.

With the group stage completed it seemed that England had checked all the relevant boxes: bafflingly below-par performances, a frenzied media stoking up anxiety back home, endless debates over the playing system. But over in Pretoria Everton's Landon Donovan had quietly added another item to the list. His last-gasp goal against Algeria simultaneously hoisted the US from the departure lounge to the top of the group while relegating England to the runner's-up spot. So instead of an African adventure against Ghana up in the Highveld, it was to the Free State next for a reunion with some old friends.

BELLVILLE RENDEZ-VOUS

THE VICTORIA AND ALFRED WATERFRONT IN CAPE TOWN IS A powerful symbol of modern South Africa. Looming cranes and the odd statuesque tanker hint at a history of maritime commerce, but look around at the boardwalk cafes, quayside restaurants and shopping malls, and it soon becomes clear that the main freight these days is human. A shining lure floating on the sparkling water of the Atlantic Ocean, the Waterfront is an open invitation to the wealthy of Gauteng and people from that other place, known in South Africa simply as 'overseas'. A mile or so inland, closer to the heart of the old town, the pentagonal castle provides a more solid, immovable testament to the historic relationship between this town clinging to the tip of Africa and the wider world. Six flags flutter above the castle wall, each representing the groups that have, at different times, staked their claim to the land.

From my place in the queue snaking up The Strand I could see the two Union Jacks separated by the pair representing the Dutch colonists. Ahead of me, further down the hill, English and German flags were predominant, but there were also stars, rainbows, the odd rising sun. The crowd was waiting patiently to file into the Grand Parade, the main World Cup 'Fanfest' in Cape Town, to witness a match referred to in the South African *Sunday Times* that morning as World War III. Well, it was a lovely day for it.

Driving into town from the suburbs, down long avenues whose trees still clung to a few crisp golden leaves, the soft winter sunshine bathed the city in a warm glow. When the wind howls and grimy damp clouds drift across the mountain, Cape Town can be grey and inhospitable, but under a blue sky with a fresh white tablecloth on the peak it is, in my view, the most beautiful city on earth. The relaxed, sunny mood in the town contrasted sharply with the needling hostilities that had been flying between the English and German press. The opening salvo came from Berlin's *BZ*: "Yes! Now we're going to get the little English girls!" *The Sun* assured them that England were now the favourites: "Das Boot is on the other foot!" The *Nuremberger Nachrichten* cut to the chase: "This is always about more than football. It also concerns things like the three most prominent Germans of all time: Karl Marx – buried in London's Highgate; Hitler and naturally, Franz Beckenbauer. England have had years of pain."

Above the hum of the crowd and the parp of vuvuzelas inside the Fanfest I heard a low murmur of discontent rumbling up through the queue; a Chinese whisper began to spread: the park was full, they had closed the gates.

Ten minutes later we were back in the car tearing out of the city bowl. We were bombing around Hospital Bend when Klose opened the scoring with a goal that was statistically beautiful – his 50th for Germany, equalling Pelé in the pantheon of World Cup marksmen – if not aesthetically so. "Total route one," was the message from SABC on the car radio, as we sped down the highway towards the twin towers at Athlone.

In days gone by radio commentators would describe in clipped tones the location of the action by reference to grid numbers mapping the pitch. These days the commentaries are less predictable – the mood swings between calm and measured during passages of midfield build-up, and urgent and shouty as an attack unfolds. As my brother-in-law carved through the traffic like a Neapolitan taxi driver, I listened in silent horror to the near hysterical commentator bawling about successive German assaults. I felt strangely helpless, as if watching the pictures would somehow afford me a greater influence on proceedings in Bloemfontein. There was a definite sense during the build-up to the game that this would be the defining moment for England at World Cup 2010. It sounded like a horror show and I was desperate to see it. Departing from the Anglo-Germanic sniping, *The Sunday Times* had offered a saucier perspective, referring to the "sadomasochistic delight" fans take in this particular fixture. Listening to this uncomfortable but compelling showdown was not enough, I had to endure the pain of watching; only then could I suffer enough to affect the outcome.

The following day the folly of this theory was pointed out to me by a man who seemed to have leapt straight from the pages of Dr Seuss – Jean-Claude, a Mauritian electrician. We were sitting in the Grand Parade watching the Dutch glide past Slovakia, the sun warmed our backs, cold beers sat on the table – a philosophical discussion was unavoidable. It opened in a prosaic manner as we exchanged our club allegiances: Jean-Claude followed Barcelona from afar; my preference aroused his curiosity.

"So, tell me about this Crystal Palace."

I provided a potted history of highlights from the past two decades. The talent that gathered around the turn of the nineties – Wright and Bright, Salako, Southgate, Coleman, Martin – only to be picked off by injury or bigger clubs. The heroic charge to the 1990 Cup Final; edging past the mighty Liverpool 4-3 in the semi, holding Manchester United 3-3 at Wembley – beyond mere fantasy football and on into the realms of full-blown, gibbering madness. United win a dull replay 1-0, sanity returns. With paradise lost, the descent begins. A young millionaire hoses £30m into the wind chasing a dream, in the process employing the laugh-out-loud funny managerial double act of Attilio Lombardo and Tomas Brolin. His final act before being dragged to the bankruptcy court is to hurl his last wad of notes at Terry Venables. Relegation follows. A new owner appears – another young millionaire – who is generous with his opinions, less so with the transfer kitty. Managers come and go, mud is slung.

The final peak on the timeline takes us to the Adam and Eve

pub in Hackney. Here you find me surrounded by West Ham fans; some have shaven heads, many are tattooed. We are watching the Championship Play-off Final, arguably the richest one-off match in world football. Through a thick fug of smoke and resentment I watch Palace scramble a goal, spectacularly against the run of play, and cling to it, like a toddler to its comfort blanket, until the final whistle. As the last few seconds ebb away and the Irons around me curse and belch bitterly at the ref, I gaze at the screen impassively and sip my pint. Like the wide-mouthed frog facing down the crocodile, I strain every sinew in my body to stop my face cracking into a broad grin. Having reached the nirvana of the Premiership the owner declares his work done, professing a growing disinterest in football and inviting offers. Press reports suggest that Colonel Gadaffi is tempted, but sadly he decides to pursue other opportunities. The business slumps into administration and casts around for saviours. Press reports suggest that P Diddy is tempted, but sadly he decides to pursue other opportunities.

That pretty much dealt with: "who?", but Jean-Claude had a tougher, supplementary question up his sleeve: why?

The best I could offer him was a faded memory from the hurly burly of a primary school playground football match. Mark Ratcliffe – a legend of such fixtures, his mastery of the bobbling tennis ball was unmatched – ghosts past, spots the red, white and blue sweatbands accessorising the cuffs of my grey jumper and remarks casually: "Palace yeah? Skill." The next thing I know it's my seventh birthday and I am unwrapping the beautiful white shirt with a single, diagonal blue and red stripe.

And then I really confessed. "I don't really support Palace. I just monitor their progress."

Jean-Claude looked appreciably baffled by this petty distinction. I tried to explain that, while they will always be my team, I rarely attend games and generally try not to become too embroiled in their business. Fans get behind their clubs in various ways. For me, with Palace it's simple: I tend to ignore them. Midway through the season that ended in the Adam and Eve, the Eagles hovered over the relegation zone, preparing to swoop majestically down into Division One. I flounced away in disgust, washing my hands of the whole sorry business, only to find them pecking and scratching at the door to the Premiership six months later.

"You see, this is the right way – let the game run its course. Everything that must happen, will happen. This is just football, you must not suffer for it."

The conversation with Jean-Claude drew me back to a train of thought that had been chugging quietly around my head since before the tournament began. If one weighs emotional investment against return, does England offer the worst value in the international football market? The recurring cycle goes something like this. Early in the tournament, an inflated sense of superiority is punctured, pricked by struggles against Algerians and Trinidadians. Miserable recriminations ensue. Later we see a barnstorming showdown with a team deemed to be of equal status and repute – often one drawn from a back catalogue of 'old enemies' with whom we have 'history', military, sporting, colonial. (Away from football, on the rugby or cricket field, a showdown with the Australians cannot pass without a muttered reference to 'the convicts'.) Too often this ends in failure. Miserable recriminations ensue. It seems that our opponents are either beneath us – It's only Slovenia for God's sake; You do know we invented this game? – or sworn foes tainted by the stigma of an earlier skirmish. Perhaps, in future, as we slap our boys on the back and send them into the fray we should, just for fun, balance our hopes with the weight of the available evidence – statistical analysis, form, that sort of thing – rather than burden the whole enterprise with the crushing weight of history.

We pulled off the highway into the Athlone Stadium car park. All was worryingly still. Some security guards wandered over: "No fan park here today, try Khayelitsha." As we roared down Mew

Way, past a world of shacks, Podolski drilled the ball between David James's ankles and into the corner of the net. In Khayelitsha we found a ragged field, a big screen, a closed gate. "Bellville," the guards assured us. "Head for the Velodrome." The Bellville Velodrome? Taxis buzzed around us, shouting destinations and hooting, the radio babbled with tales of English woe and my over-stimulated subconscious summoned up a slideshow of scenes from Sylvain Chomet's lavishly bonkers, Oscar-nominated cycling-based animation, *Belleville Rendez-vous*.

We curved back around the highway in the direction of the city, heading towards the sinking sun. Below us the townships were alive with dozens of football matches – alongside the highway, in side streets, beneath flyovers, on every scrap of unclaimed land, a pair of makeshift goalposts faced each other, separated by hordes of eager youngsters kicking up a storm of dust and sand. Dogs scuttled in and out of play, goats and horses kept a safer distance.

By the time we had reached Bellville, Upson had pulled a goal back. We parked at a rakish angle in front of a small parade of shops, leapt from the car and raced across six lanes of highway and down the hill towards the velodrome. My heart was racing – when we burst out of the car, through the window of a launderette, on a flickering TV, I had glimpsed a replay of a Frank Lampard goal. England were level and we were about to join a mob of local fans for an unmissable second half.

Wrong, wrong, wrong.

We wandered back up the hill from the deserted velodrome and found a bar. I subsequently learned that the fan parks outside of the city, in and around the townships, were only open on the days when the Green Point Stadium was staging a match. It looked like these outlying venues were not designed exclusively to create pockets of World Cup fever in the sticks, but also to limit the numbers travelling into town on match days.

We settled into a booth beneath a widescreen TV and watched

the SABC pundits, unable to hear their insights over the booming Europop. There was John Barnes mouthing sweet nothings at me; another firm favourite with my Irish gran: "Dat John Barnes, sure he has a lovely speaking voice." Now I saw the Lampard 'goal' again – the players' reactions, the cutaway to Capello's comedy double-take. I didn't need to hear the punditry: 1966 and all that – the weight of history squeezing us out of another tournament.

The second half kicked off and a chilled bottle of Amstel appeared in front of me. As I took a sip, Müller drove towards the English goal, the red sea parted, he shot, James parried then dashed out cursing his back line, and Capello – stranded many miles from the home of *catenaccio* – rose from the bench, apoplectic with rage. I placed my empty bottle back on the table. Another one of those, please.

The bar was filling fast with people keen to wring one last blast out of the weekend. Trays bearing pints of royal blue cocktails circulated, in the next booth a group puffed away on an okka pipe. Above the electronic beats there was a definite surge of vocal support whenever Germany attacked. I don't think this was motivated by anti-English feeling, just that the dash of the youthful German side was irresistible.

More beers, more naïve defending, two more German goals. Now we were in familiar territory: perceived injustice, palpable ineptitude. The knot of tension in my stomach began to unravel; the ordeal was over for another two years. History still flitted about, trying to catch the eye: a caption explained that a further German goal would avenge their 2001 drubbing; soon after, the camera fell upon two fans in blue RAF uniforms with drooping false moustaches. The game ended, the bar rang with cheers. In the days that followed, the recriminations flew from the scattergun: the players, the management, the officials, Fifa, everyone took a hit. Sitting in that bar in Bellville I settled on a simple verdict and stuck with it: the 20 minutes either side of half-time captured some of the most exciting football in the tournament; but over the 90, the better side had won.

I made my way to the gents and stood at the urinal listening to a pan-piped arrangement of *The Sound of Silence*. A brawny young man settled himself noisily into the adjacent stall. I know it's asking a lot, but try to picture David Hasselhoff circa 1987, but blonde and with a russet goatee. He stood hands on hips, hosing thunderously and beamed at me.

"Hey bru, the English were kak, ne?"

I was about to attempt a pithy retort but decided against. Partly because he was right but mainly because he had embarked on a lengthy fart that was registering its fourth key change by the time I had finished washing my hands. No more cheery vuvuzelas for England, just the mournful last post sounded on a dyspeptic slide trombone.

As we swept back down into the city bowl, the lights of Cape Town twinkled in the darkness gathering around the foothills of Table Mountain. Somewhere down in the shadows two Union Jacks hung limply, next to their Dutch counterparts. In the far distance, the wispy blanket of smog strung out above the Cape Flats was blood-red. On the car radio a local station was hosting a post-match phone-in. Erica from Claremont felt that the phantom goal situation was "horribly, horribly unfair"; Japie from False Bay wanted to talk about karma and the fifth goal from the 1966 final. We drove on into the gathering gloom heading for a city burdened by history, listening to its views about a footballing nation with a similar problem.

TWO DAYS AFTER MY BELLVILLE RENDEZ-VOUS WITH ENGLAND, I was sitting in the upper tier of the Green Point Stadium. Driven by the metronomic beat from their booming drums, the Spanish and Portuguese fans blasted their vuvuzelas in unison, sending fruity parps swirling around the circular stadium that seemed to get stuck under the lipped roof, creating a whiplash echo. "Wheee-keesh! Wheee-keesh!" Not since the Mexican Wave has a World Cup given such a star role to a non-playing cast member. Coke were way ahead of the curve, building much of their 2010 designs around the likeness between their tall slim bottle and the long, sleek horn. Hyundai took things up a level, balancing a giant vuvuzela on the brink of the unfinished flyover in the centre of Cape Town, the city's famous road to nowhere.

Filing into the magnificent new arena it was noticeable that the security checks were also carefully focussed – OK guys: any guns, any knives, any Pepsi? Around the stadiums and fan parks Fifa were rigid in their enforcement of the approved sponsors, shooing away local traders and their wares. It would have been nice to sup a Castle during a match at a South African World Cup but that was not an option. There was Bud or Bud. Before kick-off at Green Point I gulped down the king of beers, while below me the world's most expensive player was practising his free kicks, and I felt slightly underwhelmed by both. The beer was a soft froth of blandness, while Cristiano also looked more concerned with style than substance. Even during his warm-up routine the pose he adopted before striking the ball – shoulders back, deep breath – was instantly recognisable from the Nike campaign. With the round of 16 nearing its conclusion, Ronaldo was the last man standing from the lead roles in their epic World Cup commercial: Rooney was already back home tuning out the feedback from the media backlash, while Ronaldinho had not even made the Brazilian squad.

Watching Brazil's serene progress to the quarter-finals, the absence of a showy star was looking increasingly like a strength. Of course there was Kaká, but his growing influence was as the selfless provider at the heart of a cohesive team effort. The old romantics longing for the samba skills would have to rely on footage from the

1998 World Cup: the last time we saw the very best of the beautiful game – everyone getting a touch, showing off their party pieces, dancing around the airport to a Sergio Mendez soundtrack.

Watching the Iberian derby confirmed my view that 2010 would be the year of the best team rather than the best collection of individuals. The expectation amongst the Portuguese fans seemed to focus almost exclusively on Ronaldo; their Spanish counterparts delighted in heckling the poster-boy when he lingered on the ground, denied a free kick. Miguel, a Real Madrid fan sitting next to me, cackled with laughter and surreptitiously passed me a hip flask containing throat-scalding brandy. How he got that past the Coke police I will never know. I asked him how Cristiano was fitting in at the Bernabéu.

"It's OK, this is our kind of player – we like our galacticos. So, he struts around like a peacock, that's fine, we can live with that. We have to, now we have José arriving..." He laughed: "Let them all come, we will offer them whatever they want."

"But what about the future, what about the debts?" I asked.

Miguel slipped me the hipflask again. "Tranquilízate, amigo, the whole world is in debt."

The man who stood head and shoulders above the rest that evening is unlikely to appear on a Coke bottle or tube of Pringles anytime soon. The beating heart of the Spanish team personifies understatement, so much so that he has even picked up the nickname the 'anti-galactico'. Andrés Iniesta busied himself in midfield, performing the role he does so well for Barcelona – prompting and nudging, keeping the tic-tac ticking. At one point he wrong-footed three Portuguese opponents with a series of body swerves that brought to mind Clodoaldo's 1970 dance-steps.

Far below me a knot of white shirts struck up a familiar anthem, "Eng-ger-land, Eng-ger-land, Eng-ger-land." There was a pause and then: "We're shit and we know we are, we're shit and we know we are..." If only there was a World Cup for ironic self-deprecation.

The stadium announcer reported a crowd of 63,000. Gazing around the vast bowl thronging with people I felt suddenly maudlin, soaked with flat Bud and fiery Spanish brandy. I wondered again about the aftermath of this wild football fiesta. Fifa would walk away with bulging pockets thanks to their patronage of a handful of corporate heavyweights, but what about the host nation? When would Green Point draw more crowds like this to pay its bills?

Of course, there is more than one way to make a buck out of the World Cup. A couple of years ago while staying with my parents-in-law in the Garden Route town of George, I met a musician called John Pretorius. He said he hoped to use the World Cup as a springboard for recording a hit song. We sat on the lawn watching him strum his guitar and sing. My daughter Anna was wide-eyed, entranced by the show; I couldn't quite see past a gentleman of a certain age wearing leather trousers. But John had form where major world events are concerned. A veteran of the Struggle, he had celebrated Mandela's release from prison with a performance of the protest song *sekunjalo ke nako* in front of 120,000 people in the Grand Parade. Twenty years later *Ke Nako* (It's time) was reborn as a World Cup anthem and released as part of Fifa's official World Cup album. By a happy coincidence Ke Nako is also the name of a popular Japanese cooking sauce and the song became the rallying cry for the Japanese team. A few hours before I made my way over to the Green Point Stadium, John was delivering a live performance via speaker phone to the Samurai Blue ahead of their match against Paraguay. There was even talk of a recording deal with Sony; all John had to do now was check the fine print on his Fifa contract.

A SHOT IN THE DARK

Never trust a man wearing inflatable lederhosen. I learnt this golden rule for life while basking in warm, early afternoon sunshine outside a pub in Port Elizabeth called Michelle's Chinese Takeaway. We were enjoying an unsponsored beer ahead of the quarter-final between Brazil and Holland, watching a collage of citrus colours flow past as fans streamed down the hill towards the Nelson Mandela Bay Stadium. The suspect party was an obese, middle-aged man wearing a vintage Netherlands shirt over which he had contorted a number of amber balloons into a curious braces 'n' shorts ensemble. He was sitting on the pavement in front of the pub, a large bottle of Castle in one hand, an orange vuvuzela in the other, trying to catch the eye of a succession of Brazilian beauties. "Eh! Eh!" Parp! Parp! If any deigned to look his way he would raise his bottle and eyebrows, the rictus grin spreading beneath his twitching moustache revealing a yawning gap between his front teeth. It appears that the Dutch have no word for 'cad' – they should.

I had travelled up from Cape Town to stay with my brother-in-law Craig at his farm near Plettenberg Bay. From there a group of us joined a convoy of fans processing through the stunning scenery separating the Western and Eastern Capes, heading for a beautiful match: Brazil v Holland – Joga Bonito v Shexshee Football. I was still pinching myself as I took my seat in the front row of the lowest tier. No more than 25 yards away Kaká was balancing a Jabulani on his forehead. Behind me rows of brightly costumed fans were gradually working themselves up to fever pitch, bouncing a vast inflatable World Cup over their heads. Above them bright sunshine illuminated the ellipses running around the roof of the handsome new stadium, giving them the appearance of a row of tall, slender shields. Battle was about to be joined.

Despite a change to their blue kit, the Brazilians picked up where they had left off against Chile. Solid, uncompromising defending coupled with midfield industry created a platform for Kaká to conjure up chances for the frontrunners. But when Robinho scored it was not the artist that set him up but one of the artisans – the rugged Felipe Melo – sliding a pass behind the Dutch backline. The crowd around me erupted: drums banged, yellow and green flags swished through the air, a megaphone led victorious chanting over the blaring vuvuzelas. The fan sitting next to me, a coiled spring called Lubez, fell to his knees and crossed himself thrice before leaning over the railing and shouting at the celebratory Brazilian huddle: "Eh! Eh! Melo! Eh Cabrón! Eh! Eh!" At that moment, in the middle of those celebrations, on the edge of the Eastern Cape, I felt about as close to the heart of the World Cup as one could get.

Travelling through the heart of the Eastern Cape before the tournament had raised concerns similar to those I had felt while exploring the northern provinces. Once you get beyond the towns of Port Elizabeth and East London the long thin province stretches out into rural wilds – a place of natural riches but great poverty. It's easy to fly between Port Elizabeth and Durban and I wondered how the World Cup would penetrate the beautiful wilderness between the two tourist hot spots. Before and during the World Cup I witnessed some wonderful scenes depicting the world's favourite game, but the images that I return to most often are of the kickabouts on the baked-mud pitches of the Transkei.

Referring simply to the area beyond the Kei River, the Transkei is a broad sweep of sparsely populated land stretching over some 16,500 square miles. To the north it reaches as far as the Drakensberg mountains ringing the Kingdom of Lesotho, while its eastern border stretches along the Wild Coast to the seaside towns of Kwa Zulu Natal. With the country gearing up for its big event, in a moment of sleep-deprived insanity, my wife and I decided to take our six-month-old twins Tom and Sylvie for a road trip into the unknown.

We set off from the Caltex Ultra City – a complex offering petrol, fast food and basic provisions for the road; over the next two days the Caltex logo would become a familiar sight, rising in the far distance, often the only obvious sign that the last few centuries had visited the stunning, wild terrain. Soon we were rising through a softening landscape, undulating gradually around the contours of grassy hillsides. In the far distance a few head of cattle idled across acres of all-you-can-eat buffet. The odd scraggy-looking goat wandered alongside the road, oblivious to passing traffic. The sheer scale of the landscape was hard to take in; the view seemed to stretch away to the curve of the earth's surface. All I could see for miles around were rolling hills, tumbling into fertile grasslands. Scattered across this broad canvas the circular huts of the Xhosa farmers – mud, ant heaps and cow dung packed into neat rondavels, topped with a twist of thatch – were unmissable in their glowing pastel shades of pink, green, yellow and blue; like cake decorations sprinkled on to this masterpiece as a final flourish of inspired lunacy.

It soon became clear that there was a certain style to driving through the Transkei. A muscular 4x4 may look a tad excessive nosing through the London traffic – how often does one find a bullock lying across Oxford Street? – but here they suddenly looked fit for purpose. Watching these snub-nosed tanks cruise by, dragging trailers loaded with kit, I sensed a certain belligerence in their insistence on maintaining a fixed speed, irrespective of the road conditions or other users and it began to irritate me. Quite apart from somnambulant parents ferrying their precious infants, there were other road users that deserved some consideration. Pedestrians, for example. As ever, the roadsides were lined with people going about their business, travelling to work or school. Every time some impatient oaf in a beefed-up land cruiser thundered past, nudging us aside, I had to grip the wheel to avoid mowing down a happy crocodile of year fives.

Not for the first time I was struck by a sense of separation. The local people walking between villages seemed at one with their environment – lying down to rest and chat in the long grass, seeking out the shade of trees, moving at a different pace, insinuating themselves into their natural surroundings. A few yards away, cocooned in air-conditioned cells fashioned from plastic and leatherette, another group of people raced by, barrelling onward to the next oasis of petrol and Coke machines.

In mid-afternoon we stopped in Mthatha. Until a name change in 1994, 'Umtata' was the official capital of the Transkei and the central focus of trade and commerce in the area. The greater opportunities for movement and expansion that followed the fall of Apartheid have seen a slow migration of business to more prosperous areas. We were passing through town on a Friday afternoon and the preparations for the weekend were in full swing. A bustling market sprawled along the main street, oblivious to the cars edging along it. The focal point of noise and life was the taxi rank, where a large group had gathered to chat and dance to music booming out of a PA system.

Throughout South Africa the taxis form an important layer in the economic and social strata. These mini-vans – spanning the full spectrum of roadworthiness – provide an affordable option for the car-less masses, buzzing through communities, blaring their horns, shouting out destinations. Their place at the heart of everyday life brings power and influence. In the larger cities links between the taxi firms and organised crime are implicit; ugly turf wars erupt periodically. On a more positive note it is clear that without the perpetual motion of this fleet of rattling vans, large communities would soon grind to a sluggish halt.

In the absence of metropolitan subways or serviceable overland rail networks the World Cup organisers soon spotted the vital role of the taxis. A government scheme offered taxi owners sponsorship to replace their old death-traps with sparkling new models, fit for guests. Usually white or duck-egg blue, their main distinguishing features are the names and slogans printed across the windscreens – Playboy, Close Shave, Teddy Bear, Buggalugs, No Exit, Shy Guy, Prime Suspect, Second Chance – offering cryptic insights into the character of the driver and his crew.

On our way out of Mthatha we stopped for petrol on a road winding above the town centre. From my vantage point I could see the old Rotary Stadium, a basic rural venue ringed by tall trees, tucked in against a bank of scrubby bush. Under a thunderous sky it looked dark, beautiful and somehow peculiarly African. The grass seemed astonishingly green and I later discovered that the First National Bank had donated a new artificial pitch to the venue. More ambitious plans to build a brand new stadium on the edge of town as a venue for World Cup training camps soon ran into familiar-sounding problems.

Construction stalled while the apparent misplacement of R2m of start-up funds was investigated. By the end of 2008 the original budget of R100m had bloated by a further R70m. Part of this was legal fees. The proposed site was situated on land whose ownership was disputed by the local Zimbane community; a series of attempted settlements and references to the Land Claims Court followed. Looking down at the lovely old ground I hoped that, one way or another, the World Cup would hack its way through the political and financial undergrowth and find its way to Mthatha.

In late afternoon we headed for the coastal resort of Port St Johns. As we began a slow spiral back down to sea level, the landscape began to change dramatically. We left behind the sunlit grasses and trees and fell into a gloomy world where dense foliage dripped with dangling vines and pervasive creepers. The slow descent ended with a long straight drive along the bank of a wide, soupy river the colour of milk chocolate. There were few other road-users; the only notable sight was a whip-thin elderly gentleman, doffing his trilby and offering a broad grin, as he rolled past on what appeared to be a vintage Raleigh Chopper. We stopped at a handsome old guest house situated on a broad lawn in a clearing cut into the surrounding vegetation. We carried bags and babies up to a room on the first floor swathed in mosquito nets. The heat was flattening. I nipped downstairs to reception to deal with the paperwork and emitted an involuntary moan of relief when I spotted a fridge loaded with frosty beers.

We laid the babies on one of the beds, gurgling and wriggling, entranced by the whirring blades of the ceiling fan and sat out on the balcony sipping and sweating, watching the light fade over the steaming undergrowth. Nearing the end of my second bottle of Windhoek, I was drifting into idle speculation about the commercial viability of *Deliverance: the Musical*, imagining a barn-storming solo by a toothy, banjo-plucking redneck: "Squeak piggy, squeak – pass me my crossbow, Zeke…", when my wife shattered my reverie.

"We're out of nappies."

With dusk falling I walked into town, following streetlights strung between telegraph poles, heading for signs of life in the far distance with only the hoots and screeches from the surrounding forests and the distant rumble of the ocean for company. The small centre of Port St Johns rambles around a horseshoe of market stalls and basic amenities. Late on a Friday the world of commerce was giving way gratefully to the weekend festivities and I had to scramble under the half-closed shutter of the general store. Emerging with a thick pack of nappies under each arm I wandered over to the taxi rank. Music blared from the cab of a taxi tagged 'Cheeky Chops' – a curious mixture of Afrikaans accordion and booming African beats. People were dancing, shaking slowly in time to this hybrid sound, chatting and drinking. The sickly sweet aroma of dagga wafted through the heavy night air; on the periphery a pair of policemen perched on the bonnet of their car looked on benignly.

As I followed the swinging bulbs back down the main street, I spotted some brighter lights twinkling through the trees and took a diversion through a stretch of parkland. I found a handful of young boys having a kickabout on a rough pitch illuminated by some stooped, rusting floodlights. One young lad, smaller than the rest, was standing on the sideline, arms folded, observing the action with a studious frown. He greeted my approach with a solemn nod and introductions followed. Inevitably, Thulani's grasp of English was far superior to my smattering of Xhosa and we had soon begun exchanging the names of our favourite footballers.

"For me, Zidane was the man," I explained.

"Messi," responded Thulani, shaking his head mournfully and wagging a finger of self-reproach.

"Eish, I like this guy. I like this guy too much."

Even across language and cultural divides I was happy that we both opened our impromptu round of Top Trumps with the mercurial genius from our respective generations – the kind of player venerated in Italian football as Il Fantasista. Thulani shouted across to the other boys. Without looking up from his attempts to dribble past an opponent the eldest shouted something back and waved his hand. Thulani nodded, pointed to himself and then to me.

"Come."

As the penny dropped I felt a surge of excitement. The boys were playing in pairs, attacking the crooked goalframe at one end of the park. Thulani had been the odd man out, now he had a partner. Arguably. I trotted behind him onto the pitch but something didn't feel right. I looked down at the 440g packet of nappies wedged under each armpit and walked back to the touchline to lay down the burdens of parenthood.

As the boys played they maintained a running Xhosa commentary, building a stream of whoops and clicks into a final yelp naming the idol they had become: "Eh, eh, eh, yo, yo, yo – Kakaaaaaa!" Thulani and I fell swiftly into our adopted roles as Messi and Zidane. For the first five minutes my sheer exhilaration carried me along and I leapt about the pitch like a middle-aged gazelle. But all too soon the only pace I could muster was the jackhammer pounding of my heart. As I had stolen his name I decided to appropriate Zizou's style; time for some sangfroid. Rather than sprint I began to jog in a laconic, slightly aloof fashion. I would wait for the ball to arrive and then execute one of his trademark moves – coaxing in challenges only to pirouette away, leaving defenders on their backsides; casting a glance to the left, only to side-foot the ball to the right; dropping the shoulder, turning on a centime and bending a rasping shot between the angle of post and crossbar. That was the plan. In truth, I never got beyond the aloof jogging. Which soon became aloof walking. At 38 I have come to accept the fact that the window of opportunity on my career as an international footballer may be creaking shut. These days when I jab an angry finger at a televised football match and crow: "I could do better than that!" it is only true if the camera has alighted on a spectator making a messy job of eating their half-time pie.

Just when it seemed that a meaningful contribution to that evening's fixture was beyond me, Thulani scooped a perfect cross in my direction. As I watched the threadbare, puffy ball loop through the night sky I began to visualise the manner in which I would greet it. The goal was about 15 yards away at an angle of 45 degrees; the keeper was rooted to his line. Time to rescue the Zidane name, wind back the clock, retrouvé le temps. My debut competitive goal on African soil would be a classic.

The closing scenes of *Escape to Victory* follow Ossie Ardiles on a mazy dribble down the right wing which sees him mule-kick the ball over his head and that of the advancing German defender. He then chips a delightful pass into the penalty area for Pelé. As the Brazilian leaps into the super-slow-motion bicycle-kick that won the Second World War, an eerie tootle of pan pipes drifts across the shot. It may have been the wind whispering through the steaming forest around us, or possibly the beers, but as my right leg swung into a savage scythe at the ball I felt sure I could hear those pipes playing. I was in the zone, the Pelé Zone. Artistic insouciance be damned. Zinedine, sorry love, but this one is going to be an absolute screamer.

And then the lights went out.

I never did discover why. It might have been ESKOM load-shedding, or maybe the Port St Johns Municipality always cut the floodlights at that hour. At the time I was more concerned with the shooting pains searing through my left ankle. The sudden plunge into darkness had upset the balance of my meticulously judged, once-in-a-lifetime, textbook volley. Instead of belting the ball into the middle of next week my right foot swept millimetres past it, continued at high speed, and collected my standing foot. I had somehow managed to scythe myself down with a sickening challenge.

THERE WERE SOME EQUALLY UGLY TACKLES FLYING ABOUT AS I watched the Brazilians going about their business in the second half at the Nelson Mandela Bay Stadium. Perhaps certain Brazilian teams of the past might have viewed a one-goal advantage as an excuse to turn on the style and press for more. The impression I got from Dunga's troops that afternoon was that they wanted to protect what they had while trying to batter their opponents into accepting an inevitable defeat. When the Dutch equalised the aggression seemed to intensify; the Joga Bonito was nowhere to be seen as hefty specimens like Lucio, Maicon and Melo rough-housed the buzzing orange threat posed by tiddlers like Robben and Sneijder. Next to me, Lubez was scowling and screaming: "Puta! puta! puta!....", unhappy with what he was seeing. It seems we all have a somewhat idealised view of how Brazilian football should be played. Even the Dutch coach seemed a bit disappointed after the game: "If you take a look at the video you would be ashamed – ashamed for Brazilian football."

As the South Americans chased the game into the dying minutes, Maicon came over to take a corner right in front of me. There were only a handful of blue shirts in the box and I watched him bellowing angrily to the big defenders to come up and join in. It was Maicon that opened Brazil's scoring at the World Cup – a lovely shot from the touchline swerving behind the North Korean goalkeeper that many of us chose to believe was purely intentional, classic samba-style brilliance. Now here he was again, down in the same corner of the pitch, looking to lump in a cross for the big men, trying to rescue their campaign.

I guess it goes without saying that the likes of Robben and Sneijder did not feature in that park fixture up in Port St Johns, whereas Robinho, Ronaldinho, Kaká et al were all there, night after night. Of course it's unfair to burden a team with the responsibility of delivering fantasy football, but a more reasonable expectation also rests at their feet – as role models for millions of impressionable kids watching their every move. After the game Dunga felt his side had "failed to maintain rhythm". In reality the problem wasn't the lack of smooth flowing moves, it was the ugly sharp edges. Shortly before the final whistle, during a tussle with a Dutch defender in the corner closest to us, Kaká threw out an instinctive, irritated forearm. It missed the defender's forehead by inches, but I could visualise the nasty scene that would have unfolded: the player hits the deck, an angry mob gathers around the referee, Kaká is shown a red card and trudges out of the tournament in disgrace. While I felt incredibly privileged to see the world's greatest players at such close quarters, I couldn't help thinking that the version of Kaká that existed in the imagination of the boys up in the Port St Johns Recreation Ground was probably more reliable.

THE BOYS HELPED ME UP AND SENT ME HOBBLING ON MY WAY TO our guest house. Back in our room Tom was chuntering restively, threatening to rouse the others and I decided to take him for a stroll to see if I could loosen up my self-imposed injury.

The garden was bordered by dense vegetation but I spotted a path heading a few hundred yards along the shoreline towards the twinkling lights of another establishment. The moon was a vast, silvery disc, beautifully full, illuminating rocks, sand and the frothing waves through the trees to our left. Tom loved it, wide eyes darting left and right, reaching for dangling creepers and jumping at squawks and rustles from the undergrowth.

About 100 yards down the path, the still night was broken suddenly by the crackle and noisy "pop, pop, pop" of fireworks. I found a small break in the trees and took a few steps down towards the beach, hoping for a glimpse of the show. Although the noises seemed close by there was nothing to see. As I turned to rejoin the path I heard a sharp zinging sound, more rustling and saw a group of shadows race past. We carried on our way but soon became aware of a further commotion ahead of us: urgent shouts and flashlight beams. By now Tom was in double-take heaven, his little head whipping from side to side, grinning and gurgling approvingly. Four armed policemen bustled up and urged us to return to our guest house. They were pursuing a band of Mozambican burglars, well known to them, who often used the path as an escape route after swooping on a beachfront establishment. The 'fireworks' we had heard were their warning shots; one of the policemen claimed to have winged a suspect. Eish.

Back in the car the next morning we followed the long, straight road along the soupy river and stopped at a garage for petrol. Unlike the homogenised Caltex complexes on the main road, this was a local concern set next to the ghost of an old bookstore. Crumbling broken walls were being dragged slowly into the surrounding foliage by leafy tendrils and spidery vines. Looking further into the ruin I could see shadowy nooks and darkened corners. As I filled the car a succession of men wandered into the building, bottles swinging by their sides. Walking into the shop to settle up, I stumbled across the tail-end of an ugly scene between the cashier and a wild-eyed, shaven-headed man. From what I could make out, he seemed convinced that she was in league with Satan.

I returned to the car keen to get moving but caught a familiar odour rising from the back seat. There were no facilities, not even a stretch of grass, so I changed Sylvie on the boot, wedging her in place with an otherwise pointless spoiler. A young guy in a battered bakkie, overloaded with wooden crates full of screeching chickens, pulled up and headed for the remains of the old bookshop. Soon after, I could hear angry voices and the jarring sound of breaking glass. The budget exorcist was still haunting the shop, grinning maniacally, preaching damnation and casting interested glances in our direction. Somewhere in the distance a siren wailed and fireworks popped. Have I ever changed a nappy faster? I don't believe I have.

We climbed up and away from the riverbed on a road winding through trees shrouded in mist. The morning broke softly through light cloud cover, as we cruised through miles of juicily green pasture. The roads were pleasantly bereft of the chaos of taxis and trucks; the solitude was uplifting.

We passed through a series of country towns – Flagstaff, Lusikisiki, Bizana – small communities, one barely distinguishable from the next. Pedestrians bustled all over the road, taxis hooted; churches, shibeens and Boxer Superstores offered the necessities for everyday life. We stopped in Bizana to pour petrol into the car and milk into the babies. An unremarkable rural town, Bizana is the birthplace of two key figures in South Africa's recent history: Oliver Tambo and Winnie Madikizela-Mandela.

It was on the football pitch at Fort Hare University that Tambo became acquainted with Nelson Mandela, beginning a lifelong friendship that saw them take up leading roles in the ANC and establish a legal practice in Johannesburg to represent those disenfranchised by Apartheid. The link between football and Mandela's ex-wife drags us into darker territory.

Married to Mandela in 1958, the 'Mother of the Nation' became a figurehead for the Struggle movement during his long imprisonment. But while her husband had preached force against the government, aiming to sabotage the machinery of Apartheid, during the 1980s Winnie became increasingly associated with violence and intimidation against individuals. In the paranoid climate during the State of Emergency, police-informants, *impimpis*, were seen as the lowest form of life. During a speech in the township of Munsieville in 1986 she infamously stoked the fires: "Together, hand in hand, with our boxes of matches and our necklaces we shall liberate our country." The reference to matches and necklaces alluded to the practice of torching petrol-soaked tyres hung around the necks of informants.

What began as a group of young men gathered in her house under her protection became a lawless gang of thugs under the banner of the Nelson Mandela Football Club. The Club's reign of intimidation in Soweto came to a head in 1989 with the abduction of four young boys, their subsequent torture, and the murder of 14-year-old Stompie Moeketsi. The ugly details dribbled out years later during the Truth and Reconciliation Commission hearings, as the Football Team's 'coach' Jerry Richardson gave his evidence: "I slaughtered him like a goat...I put the shears through Stompie's neck. They went to the back ... I killed Stompie under instructions of Mami."

In all, 18 killings were linked to the Nelson Mandela Football Club. When Winnie made her appearance before the Truth and Reconciliation Commission it drew the biggest gallery for any hearing but produced little further evidence. The Commission's final report notes: "It is regrettable that Ms Madikizela-Mandela did not use the hearings as a forum to take the Commission and the Nation into her confidence in order to shed light on the circumstances that resulted in the chaos and violence that emanated from her household. This would have assisted in the process of separating wild allegation from the morass of claims made against her."

Despite subsequent convictions for fraud and theft, Madikizela-Mandela remains a popular figure, notably with the poorest sections of society. When the roster for the 2009 National Elections was announced she was named in fifth spot on the ANC electoral role; a powerful indicator of grass-roots support.

We drove out of Bizana back into the wide, open space. The only signs of life were healthy-looking cattle roaming in small packs coaxed on by astonishingly young boys armed with nothing but reed-like sticks. Sometimes when we stopped to let them cross the road, the boys would approach the car, their solemn young faces creasing with hope – "Zwitz? Zwitz?" – and we would delve into the glove box, grabbing a handful of something sugary. I marvelled at their self-reliance. Where did they live? What did they live on? Who taught these boys to look after animals? Crucially, who looked after them?

The American comedian Rich Hall describes his native Montana as the kind of place where, if your dog makes a run for the hills, you can monitor its progress for the next three days from the comfort of your front porch. The Transkei gave me the same kind of feeling. From its uplands, ridges and heights the view stretched away forever. As we followed the curves and dips of the landscape, far below us we could just make out the tiny figures, now sucking happily on their zwitz, tramping through this endless wild landscape.

Watching their progress I had to repress a surge of anxiety, as I inadvertently transposed my parental neuroses onto an entirely different culture. Back in our world, faced with an overwhelming amount of choice and advice, we agonised endlessly over the hypoallergenic, organic minutiae in providing for the needs of our children. I once spent an hour dithering over which car seat to buy for Anna, knowing deep down they all had identical safety ratings and that I was, in fact, debating whether she would prefer one with a turquoise or cerise trim. In an environment like the Transkei, the simplicity of life narrows the choices and potential dangers down to those that sit closest to the fulcrum between survival and disaster.

A few miles out of Bizana, as we rolled into mid-afternoon, I spotted a series of crooked sticks breaking the horizon and as we got closer I realised that we were passing a number of rustic football pitches, spread across several acres. I counted a dozen sets of goal frames – just knobbly wooden poles nailed together, no two the same.

The sight of so many pitches lying silently fallow dragged my mind back to London, E9. Our flat in Homerton was situated a short walk from the Hackney Marshes, a generous expanse of grass on the edge of the Lea Valley said to contain Europe's largest collection of football pitches. Despite its proximity to the overpopulated suburbs of East London, the Marshes are usually deserted; a perfect spot for some peace and solitude. Approaching it through the backstreets feels a bit like wandering towards the coast; catching a stiff breeze gusting across the open space, hearing the gulls wheel and screech overhead. Unusually for London it feels peaceful, undiscovered.

All that changes on Sunday mornings as tranquillity gives way to noisy emotion. Screaming and shouting, sweating and belching, men of all shapes, sizes, colours and creeds join in a communal purge, running off the excesses of Saturday night and the stresses of the past week. Walk past a group in their half-time huddle and you will see many things – hammy, tattooed forearms dragged across sweaty brows, bullets of sinuous phlegm shot to the turf, puce-faced men desperately trying to summon enough puff to take a meaningful drag on their cigarettes. Most of all you will see intensity. During the next 45 minutes they want to tuck something away to see them through the coming week. A peach of a pass, a scything tackle, a wonder strike, a super save, a nutmeg, a spot of handbags.

A free kick chipped delicately from the verdant carpet of the San Siro into the Juve net is a world away from an angry toe-punt down at the Marshes that ricochets off an ample backside before dribbling over a mud-sodden goal-line. Try telling that to the scorer, Dave, an 18st scaffolder from Barking. Go on, I dare you.

On Sunday mornings Hackney Marshes are alive with the sound of humanity laid bare – outrage, despair, anger, mockery, delight. An ambulance is always on stand-by, ostensibly to cope with sporting injuries, but also to hoover up the rest: fisticuffs at full time or the aftermath of an impulsive swing at the ref. I suspect that many of the dads that kick and scream away their Sunday mornings would hammer their sons if they saw them carry on like that during school matches.

If one of the duties of a World Cup is to promote footballers as role models then the first day of the quarter-finals was Black Friday. Having watched Brazil lose playing ugly we hurtled back through the darkness to the farm to watch the evening fixture. With dogs slumbering on rugs in front of a crackling fire and a bottle of Bushmills on the table, we settled down for a showdown between the heroes and the villains. South Africans swiftly adopted 'BaGhana BaGhana' as the new home nation, while Uruguay's theatrical diving and elimination of the real home nation quickly cast them as the new pantomime rogues. The country, the whole continent, had swung behind the Black Stars – a huge weight of expectation had shifted on to new shoulders. Sulley Muntari's skimming thunderbolt started the party for the 85,000 fans in Soccer City and when Asamoah Gyan stepped forward to take a penalty in the final minute of extra time, the happy ending looked secure. Perhaps that was the problem. After the game George Weah bemoaned the fact that the Ghanaians were celebrating their winner before it had been put away. Gyan's strike was true but even weighted down with the hopes of an entire continent the Jabulani somehow managed to soar over the crossbar and disappear into the shadows of the stand;

a shot in the dark that silenced Soccer City. There was a horrible inevitability about the ensuing penalty shoot-out. In the days that followed Oscar Tavarez, the Uruguay coach, was at pains to point out that his side had stayed within the rules. True. Suarez handled the ball on the goal-line – red card, off he went. But his unrestrained celebrations when Gyan missed and subsequent claim to be the "real hand of God" left a sour taste. These pictures and stories travelled all over the world; for the more impressionable a window into a world of cynical football had creaked open.

Towards the end of our journey through the Transkei I spotted something that looked suspiciously like the opposite end of the scale. As we left Bizana behind I spied another pitch, set apart from the original dozen. Here the lopsided goalposts were daubed in the bright paint of the Xhosa huts – eye-catching stripes of yellow, turquoise, pink and sky blue. A few miles further on we hit the back of a queue waiting to be allowed through some roadworks. I walked away from the car looking for a handy spot to relieve myself. Although I must have had the thick end of 40,000 acres of open land stretching before me, I dithered Britishly, looking for the perfect bush, traipsing ever further from the road. As I returned two young boys, I would say no more than ten years old, were coming the opposite way, leading some caramel-coloured cows through the long grass. They smiled warmly as we met, and I found half a Milo bar in the side pocket of my shorts. Attempts at further communication were limited to eager smiles and nods. The striped goalposts were still visible, across the plains, catching the glow of the falling sun and I pointed towards them, work-shopping a ludicrous mime of a man painting with a strained, quizzical expression. The smaller of the two finally put us all out of our misery.

"Soccer, beeg match." He pretended to hold a trophy aloft.

Ah. So this was the special pitch, for cup finals and the like. How lovely it must be to see your shot sail between those posts, to win a big game.

He pointed towards me: "You like soccer?"

I nodded and explained that I was from England, threw in Crystal Palace – blank expressions, a long shot – and then fell back on some star names. Even here, in the middle of nowhere, the globalised Premier League brand was instantly recognisable.

The boy smiled: "It's too much, I like these guys: Lampard, Gerrard, Rooney. I like this. In England, soccer, it is the best."

I shook my head sadly and wagged my finger. "No, not the best. *Here* is the best. Look." I pointed towards the far distant fields: "Here you guys have got rainbows for goalposts!"

They grinned, shrugged, and walked on through the endless grasslands, coaxing their little herd along with whistles and sharp calls, tiny figures in a vast, shrinking world.

A LESSON IN COACHING

Too often footballers are unfairly dismissed as an uncultured breed. Take Ian Rush's observation that he struggled to settle in Italy because it was like living in a foreign country. The chortling press failed to spot Rushy's sly nod down to L.P. Hartley; at Juventus the former Liverpool star had found a team in decline, haunted by the ghosts of their past success. Similarly the barbs that followed Glenn Hoddle's "I have never heard a minute's silence like that", overlooked his obvious devotion to the avant-garde compositions of John Cage. So Stuart Pearce could see "the carrot at the end of the tunnel"; give him a break already, the lad obviously likes his Dalí. (Either that or he's a keen organic gardener.) "If history repeats itself, I should think we can expect the same thing again." Tactical nous from Terry Venables, chalking up a crafty cyclical formation, eschewing the Marxist theory of pushing tragedy up front, leaving farce floating in the hole.

Standing in the middle of a field watching endless replays of Luis Suarez's goal-line intervention against the Ghanaians, I began to doubt the veracity of Tel's sage observation. History had repeated itself – a World Cup quarter-final featuring sky-blue South Americans; a critical handball; an attempt to shift blame on to a higher power – but could we really expect the same thing again? Maradona followed his sleight of hand in 1986 with a sublime goal. There would be no redemption for Suarez; the handball remained his most significant touch in the tournament. I was watching these pictures in the Rosemoor Stadium, a multi-purpose venue situated in the heart of the townships on the outskirts of George. The stadium consisted of a large field with a single grandstand surrounded by a cement wall topped with coils of barbed wire. Thick wooden rugby posts sat at either end of the field while in the centre a rectangular strip of mud, dry and cracked like the hide of an elephant, promised cricket in the summer. Like many local stadia in South Africa, Rosemoor offered more than mere athletic pursuits; this was a meeting point, a place for the local community to come together. They were gathering on that particular afternoon to see history repeat itself – Argentina and Germany were at it again. Setting aside a parochial English obsession with the 'Hand of God', 1986 was memorable for producing one of the best World Cup Finals ever seen; four years later the same two sides served up a stinker.

Twenty years on, the make-up of the teams had a vaguely familiar look and feel. Germany were building momentum based around a neat, clean passing game that was, clichéd though it sounds, ruthlessly efficient. For Argentina, their entire game-plan for the tournament depended on one man, their mercurial No10. Messi? No, silly, Maradona. It is often said that one of the traits of a great coach is their ability to take the pressure off the players by drawing the glare of the media spotlight on to themselves. In Diego's case I suspect that this was more a natural instinct than a lesson learnt in a coaching manual. His erratic stewardship of his nation's qualifying campaign and uncomplicated approach to a critical press – "suck it and carry on sucking" – was a good story even before he arrived in South Africa. And they just kept on coming. It is another accepted wisdom of modern coaching that the division between success and failure is a hairline; no stone should be left unturned in terms of preparation. On arriving in Pretoria, no doubt envisaging long evening sessions sitting in state musing on tactics, Maradona ordered a bespoke throne for his quarters. The local manufacturer declared it to be "the best toilet seat in the world". The Argentina boss also reached out to the nearby football community, inviting players from a local youth side to come and visit the camp, each performing seat-warming duties by way of a payback. Now I made that last bit up, but would you have known? When he wasn't shopping for world-class dunnies, Diego was having a pop at fellow legends – Platini and Pelé got short shrift, the latter being advised to "go back to the museum".

While the world's media focussed their attention on the Argentine coach it was clear from the reaction of the kids assembled at Rosemoor where their interest lay. A montage of Messi in full flow drew the biggest cheer from the crowd inspiring the MC to invite an excited crew of boys on to the stage to show off their favourite Messi tricks and, of course, goal celebrations. Soon the platform was a chaos of keepy-uppy and breakdancing. The joy on the faces of the performers and crowd was a delight. The Japanese squad had been based in George and the walls of Rosemoor were covered in bright, colourful pictures and slogans designed by the local schoolchildren, welcoming their guests: "Show Dem! Proud hosts!", "2010 Feel the Vibe". SABC's World Cup slogan was the simple but effective: "Feel it" – it was wonderful to see the football community in George getting a real feel for this great celebration of the game.

In the distance I could see the playing fields over at the Lawaai Kamp township on the outskirts of town. Before the World Cup began I spent a memorable day there watching local teams contest their own version of the biggest tournament around: a play-off for the right to join the bottom rung of the national league. I had been to watch a game here some years earlier and the scene was largely unchanged by the passage of time. The playing surface was still rough as hell, with twin bare patches bulging out from each goalmouth conjoined by an umbilical strip of dirt running through the spine of the pitch. These solidified slicks offered players the worst of all worlds: scratch the surface and the mud was sticky, above that a dusting of grit and sand was ready to lacerate thighs and knees. A handful of hefty cows mooched around nibbling the patchy grass. I remembered wooden goalposts years ago, skewed by repeated butts of curiosity from the cattle. Now they were metal, crooked and bent, with dents around their base. The cows looked slightly dazed.

The tournament was due to start at eleven o'clock. It was a quarter to; the odds on a prompt start were long. The pitches occupied a sunken stadium on a patch of land trapped between the borders of the township and a flyover bisecting the highway. Above and below the roads were busy with Saturday morning trade: vast laundry bags teetered on heads, makeshift trolleys clattered past, taxi drivers bibbed and bawled. By contrast, the pitches looked quiet and forlorn. There was little to suggest that a major football event was about to kick off. I could see a white object covering the centre spot of the farthest pitch but it didn't look like a ball. I wandered over for a closer look. No, definitely not a ball: it was a 1988 Toyota Corolla.

A handful of guys were milling around, chatting and smoking. I tried them with the password.

"Dangerous Darkies?"

There were frowns and then slow signs of recognition; they gestured towards a little group gathered on the far side of the pitch. Following further enquiries I arrived in front of Lalas, coach of the Dangerous Darkies, completing a journey that had taken several decades.

My wife's family had moved to George in the early seventies when my father-in-law accepted the task of establishing the English school in the town. When one considers that around this time students were being shot on the streets of Soweto for protesting against Apartheid's insistence on Afrikaans schooling, and that George was the constituency of PW Botha (the man who led the National Party in defending its regime against the growing clamour of international dissent), this was a challenge with a keen political edge. My mother-in-law chose to spend much of her time volunteering as an English teacher in the black school and contesting forced removals at Lawaai Kamp. As a family staunchly opposed to the Apartheid regime with a son establishing a growing profile in anti-government student politics, they lived in "interesting times". There were regular home visits from the security forces, poison pen letters and a permanent tap on the phone. Perhaps worst of all was the bogus police call to my mother-in-law, its flat tone explaining that her husband had been killed in a road accident. Enough stories to fill their own book.

Several years ago, returning to the school at Lawaai Kamp, my mother-in-law met the caretaker Simon Quotu, who mentioned a group of young men he had pulled together into a football team: the Dangerous Darkies. Lalas was their coach and I found him in an agitated state. His goalkeeper could not make it, beaten at the near post by a Saturday job at Pennypinchers. Phone calls were made and texts sent as the whereabouts of the other players was established. A young guy in a Sundowns shirt strolled up and had a quiet word with Lalas. Suddenly the pressure was off. It seemed that the Darkies' first-round opponents, United Brothers, may not be coming either. A team from the local youth prison, a mix-up with the day-release papers had grounded them. All around us players, coaches and fans were drifting slowly into the bowl of rough ground housing the pitches. A few of the Darkies boys arrived, solemn youths in a black and gold kit. Lalas explained that when he had been "retrenched" by the local McCain factory he had received the team strip in lieu of redundancy money. Wandering around I picked up the names of other teams – All Brick Brothers, Diego Masters, Young Killers, Heaven Stars – evoking a mix of fantasy and harsh reality. Prior to their match the last of these sunk to their knees in a muddy goal mouth, joined hands and bowed their heads. Lalas nodded approvingly,

"This is why these guys need soccer; it gives focus, something to be proud of."

He told me how his schooling had been lost – dyslexia misinterpreted as disinterest – and that he had been heading down the wrong track before the discipline of playing organised football had dragged him back from the brink. Now as a coach he was trying to pass on the lessons learnt.

We were joined by a portly gentleman carrying a clipboard – the local SAFA representative overseeing the running of the tournament. He and Lalas had faced each other in their playing days and they fell into fond reminiscences about past skirmishes. It transpired the Darkies coach had acquired his nickname from Alexi Lalas, the first US player to appear in Serie A, more recently famous as the man that signed David Beckham for LA Galaxy.

"This guy used to kick me nice and hard," chortled the SAFA man, poking a finger into Lalas's chest. "Eh, man: rugged," he added, rolling the 'r' halfway around the pitch.

"And this guy was a fast centre forward in those days." Lalas lifted his friend's clipboard to reveal a tightly-packed ball of easy living. "Yessirs, can you believe it?"

The man from SAFA confirmed that United Brothers would not be coming, giving the Dangerous Darkies a bye to the next round. Quite where that left them, I could not say. By then many different groups of players in various kits were milling around the pitches and it was all pretty confusing. Another ghost from Lalas's playing days drifted up – a well-built, handsome man with a bald head and a slow, broad grin. Lalas solemnly described him as the best player of their generation, while the big man raised his palms in protest. He was called Mxolisi but spared me the task of trying to wrap my tongue around that with a "you can call me Ace". I sat with him watching a game from behind one of the goals. It turned out he was the chairman of one of the teams in action, Young Blues. I asked Ace what he enjoyed about working with young players.

"Somewhere in all of this," he gestured towards the rough pitches surrounded by players in different team colours, "maybe you have the next Benni or Lucas – you just don't know it yet. If we don't go looking, we won't find them. All we can do is get these boys a trial with a bigger club, then it's up to them to show what they can do."

On the neighbouring pitch the coaches were shouting and screaming; Ace observed his charges quietly, calmly. I suspect that he had worked out that there was little point chastising players for their mistakes on such a capricious surface. Depending on whether it hit grass, sand or mud the ball bounced, skidded or died on the pitch. The players were battling the ground beneath their feet as much as each other.

A pass rolling across even turf is a straightforward proposition; trap, look up, move it on. Here the first task was to deploy thigh, shin or boot to tame the bobbling, dancing ball. I could see how pitches like this schooled the Southern African style of play, a style that steps deftly along the fine line between triumph and disaster. During the early nineties, in the Ghanaian Tony Yeboah, Leeds United had a player that exemplified this approach. He never seemed to quite have the ball fully under control, but dragged it forwards nevertheless, kicking and screaming. Once the goal hoved into view he would release his struggling captive with a sickening thump. A few millimetres either way and the approach looked clumsy as possession was lost or the strike disappeared swirling into the stand. But when it came off – a crazy-legs juggling act, followed by a thunderbolt into the roof of the net – it was the stuff of comic book fantasy. Down the M1 at Highfield Road, Peter Ndlovu was delighting and exasperating Coventry fans with similar outbursts of sporadic genius. A few years later the Liberian George Weah appeared at AC Milan and ran amok through the league that prides itself on defensive solidity. One effort against Verona saw him travel the length of the San Siro field, slaloming his way through the opposing hordes – barging, swerving, stumbling, but somehow keeping hold of the ball – before drilling it past the keeper. An anathema to the controlled order of *calcio*, the Southern African all-or-nothing playing style seems to reflect the way the game is learned: on hopeless pitches, on the edge.

The Young Blues match ended in a draw and went straight into a penalty shoot-out. In the absence of nets hanging from the mangled goal frames, confusion and honesty squared up to each other. Was that in? The nods have it. Eventually it came down to the fifth Young Blues penalty-taker; a goal would secure their passage to the next round. He placed the ball carefully on the spot – an island of tufty grass in a river of mud – and took a few paces back. I wish I could tell you what happened next, but I honestly don't know. The young man jogged forward, raised his right leg to shoot, and then in the blink of an eye, collapsed forward, jamming down on the ball with his left boot. The keeper was as dumbfounded as I was; scrabbling across to cover his left post, he watched from his knees helplessly as the ball looped lazily towards the top right-hand corner. The delicate ting it registered on grazing the angle of post and crossbar added to the still, Zen-like quality of the moment, quickly shattered by noisy delirium as the scorer was mobbed by his teammates. I looked across at Ace, my brow furrowed, bottom lip hanging limply. He was grinning broadly, rolling out a deep, rich chuckle.

"Eh, he's a cheeky boy that one."

I wandered back over to the Dangerous Darkies camp and met another of their coaches, Sidney. A small figure in a neat, olive-green tracksuit, he frowned earnestly when discussing the plans he had for the team. Down the coast at Knysna Bafana FC he had come close to making a breakthrough into the bigger leagues. As we spoke, one of his former Knysna teammates, Thabo September, was sitting atop the PSL with Supersport United.

Sometimes in South Africa one hears the phrase "African Time", often accompanied by rolling eyes and a knowing derisory chuckle. Looking around the chaotic scene in Lawaai Kamp that morning

I saw a shambles, but a triumphant, heroic shambles. Teams were unavailable, stuck in prison; individual players were incarcerated in taxis making their way in from town having escaped their Saturday jobs. At either end of the threadbare pitches cattle nosed around the netless, bent goalposts. Coaches that had missed their own chances reinvested time, skill and even their redundancy cheques in the next generation. An empty plastic milk bottle, stamped flat, provided the linesman with his flag. I had just seen a wonder goal. Like I say, a heroic shambles.

THE SHAMBLES ENGULFING THE ARGENTINE DEFENCE WAS LESS heroic as Klose and Müller wandered through it at will, set up by the lightning-fast counter attacks engineered by their team – a well-oiled machine, powered by the collective drive of its component parts. By contrast, the two cogs turning the Argentine wheel were spinning helplessly out of control. As his team fell further behind Messi took on yet more responsibility, buzzing around the well-ordered German defence, desperate to find an opening. On the touchline Diego was coming to the boil, marching up and down in his shiny grey suit, waving despairing arms. At one point, as he prepared to make changes, exasperated with the 11 on the pitch, you half expected him to tug off the tie, shrug off the jacket and trot on to sort out the whole mess himself.

At Lawaai Kamp, Lalas and Sidney had clearly accepted the fact that their playing days were behind them and adopted a more conventional approach to coaching, leading their boys through a series of carefully-prepared warm-up routines. Over on the neighbouring pitch the match had paused to permit a lively debate over the referee's decision to award a free kick on the edge of the penalty area. Once the dust had settled a tall, louche figure stepped forward to send a delicious curler into the top right-hand corner. Waving away onrushing teammates, he dashed to where the corner flag should have been to enact a carefully-rehearsed dance routine. The flapping elbows and jerky nods synergised so beautifully with the legend emblazoned across his chest – *Funky Fried Chicken* – I dared to wonder if this was a contractual requirement of the sponsorship deal.

Sidney explained that a complex sequence of byes and seeding arrangements had left the Darkies on the brink. If they could win their match that afternoon a place in the cup play-off awaited and with it the promise of elevation to the national league. It seemed remarkable that here, in this field, the road to a meeting with Pirates and Chiefs began. Standing in their way were Young Blues, the biggest fish in this local pond. Watching the Blues going through their pre-match routines they looked the part, well-organised and physically more developed than the other teams on display. One figure in particular, their No14, caught the eye; shaven-headed with ox-like shoulders, a man among boys. Sidney explained that this guy had recently returned from a trial with Supersport United. I watched as he trotted behind the goal to retrieve a ball; a few feet away a huge cow the colour of milk chocolate was munching her way through what looked like an old telephone directory. Questions raced through my mind. How can talent courted by the team at the top of the Premier League be playing here? Is this grass-roots development? Where's the grass?

Lalas introduced me to some of the players. I shook hands with Drogba, nodded to Figo – as ever the idols were borrowed from elsewhere. I couldn't help hoping that even if Bafana Bafana fell short of uniting the country behind their World Cup challenge, they would at least unearth a local gem to catch the eye of the next generation of South African fans.

Despite a howling wind the game quickly found its rhythm, two teams familiar with each other's style and system, probing, fencing, looking for the opening. The Young Blues' No14 began to look frustrated – the grimaces, outstretched arms and shakes of the head, rather like Diego pacing the line at the Green Point Stadium, this young guy had known better times and could not understand where they had gone.

I glanced over at the game on the neighbouring pitch. In a grassless goalmouth a seething mass of arms and legs struggled to make sense of it all. Eventually the ball – a lovely old-style black and white panelled affair – looped away to the edge of the area. It fell to a young man with sawn-off dreadlocks who calmly executed the finish I had dreamed of as the lights went out in Port St Johns: cushioned on the thigh, volleyed mercilessly into the goal off the underside of the bar. Ting. In a world of netless goals the metallic report adds a sense of certainty, of validity, that fresh air cannot provide. A spiteful column of wind swirled across the playing fields. The goal celebrations were lost in a cloud of dust – a joyous confusion of hugs, back slaps and high fives, in the midst of which someone was dutifully performing the funky fried chicken.

The stalemate on our pitch reached half-time. The players encircled the diminutive figure of Sydney: "OK gents, listen up." His analysis was sharp and incisive; he singled out key confrontations on the pitch and briefed the individuals concerned as to how they might prevail. Everyone listened. Then a few chipped in with views and observations. One young man, a tall, elegant central defender, noted his opposite number's propensity to carry the ball too far, leaving his partner exposed to a counter attack. It was hugely impressive – the clean discourse contrasted sharply with my previous experience of half-time team-talks; generally an unhealthy festival of recriminations, cigarette smoke and sickening belches. I had been scribbling on my pad during the first half and someone asked me for my views. I glanced in panic at the pages flapping in the wind, catching glimpses of odd phrases: "Very windy", "Funky Fried Chicken!"

"Well, their keeper's a pretty fat lad, try him with a few early shots aimed at the posts."

Thank you Arsene, that will be all.

It was time for the restart. Some of the players were lashing torn boots back together with masking tape, others gulping at water delivered by a small boy struggling under the weight of two Stoney Ginger Beer bottles, filled from a tap in the township. The players jogged back on to the pitch; the empty water bottles thrown back to the touchline caught the wind and sailed for miles.

A wave of noise dragged my attention back to the game. The eloquent central defender had called it right – his opposite number messed up in midfield, leaving an inviting channel for Drogba to ghost through, advancing on the remaining defender. Thankfully my instinctive cry of "early shot, fat keeper!" was carried away on the wind. Drogba drew the defender diagonally across the penalty area before side-footing the ball to Figo to slip past the marooned keeper. They had worked the overlap beautifully. The figures hunched along the wall stumbled to their feet and cheered.

The Darkies closed ranks, hoping to cling to their slender lead. Their players began to tumble to the ground, trying to disrupt the flow of the Blues' riposte and fritter away precious minutes. On the touchline Lalas played a supporting role in the charade; as Drogba collapsed in the centre circle, knocked down with a feathery challenge, the coach bellowed: "Eh reffy, that's a nasty one there man – that's a cree-mee-nel offence!" The Darkies' lack of ambition demanded waves of attack from Young Blues and a siege had soon developed.

A series of Young Blues corners eventually coaxed their keeper up into the opposing penalty box. Finally, the inevitable happened. Amidst a mêlée of flailing arms and legs the ball suddenly squirted into the Darkies' goal. Screams and hoots from the Blues as they enveloped the scorer, gradually became angry shouts and curses as someone spotted an old plastic milk bottle, stamped flat, flapping in the wind on the far touchline. No goal. From the resulting free kick Darkies began to play keep-ball, rolling nonchalant passes along their backline, safe in the knowledge that God was smiling on them that day. I peered over the fence back into the township; churchgoers were venturing into the streets, their smarts hats and ties flapping in the wind.

The casual clockwork passing around the Darkies defence suddenly went horribly wrong, forcing the left-back into a hasty, rather wild clearance. As he let fly with a meaty punt the onrushing Blues striker leapt into its path, receiving its full anger in his groin. Eyes bulging, he sank to the turf, cradling his tenderised testicles. His colleague, the No14, collected the loose ball and glided towards the last man. He made to shoot, the defender showed his number – eager no doubt to avoid his own lusty blow to the gonads – the striker ghosted past and rolled the ball through the legs of the abandoned keeper. A touch of class from a young man dreaming of better things. As soon as the Darkies kicked off the referee blew his whistle.

At full time in Cape Town the Germans celebrated a historic victory and looked forward to creating yet another chapter in their epic World Cup story. The road ahead for Argentina looked uncertain – would anyone back home dare suggest that the timid showing by their talented players was a consequence of the overbearing influence of the coach? That perhaps the past was Maradona but the future was Messi? Three days after the match the Lower Chamber of the Argentine Congress debated a bill calling for the erection of a statue honouring Maradona. I guess you don't mess with the gods.

Later that evening we headed down to an open-air restaurant on the beach for an all-you-can-eat seafood bonanza in honour of my father-in-law's birthday. As a coach, he left Diego standing: "Listen Richard, pace yourself, go easy on the potbrood, and don't fill up on sweet potato or you'll never even make it to the crayfish tails ..." Next to a long trench housing a raging fire there was a small bar constructed out of drift wood, topped with a thatched roof.

Behind it what can only be described as a salty old sea-dog was lining up drinks, a fixed grin creasing his leathery face.

"Wine or beer, Meneer?" he shouted over the deafening boom of the ocean smashing into the rocks behind him.

"Wine please."

"Vie zer wine?" he asked.

"Well, you know, I had a couple of beers watching the match, so I just fancy a bit of a change," I explained.

"No, vie-zer wine, *weisser* wine, *Riesling.*"

"Oh weisser, sorry, yes please, white wine, sorry." I spluttered into Fawlty overdrive.

"Good match eh? – yah, it was a *banger!*"

It turned out he had washed up in South Africa a decade or so ago after spending many years piloting ships in and out of his native port of Hamburg. He waxed lyrically about the Keegan years and wondered what had happened to English football.

"Ah but losing to this German side is not so bad – hey, at least it wasn't penalties ..."

A PENALTY SHOOT-OUT STOOD BETWEEN THE DANGEROUS Darkies and a place in the national league. Lalas pulled his men, me included, into a huddle, trying to make himself heard over the howling gale and heavy breathing of his shattered players. Whenever I watch this moment on television – usually it is England players trudging tiredly into the departure lounge of a major tournament – I always imagine a level of reticence when the call goes up for volunteers. Not with these guys, they were arguing for the right to step up.

The mountains had completely disappeared behind a sullen wall of murky cloud. The wind was spraying grit and sand sideways across the pitch. Prior to taking their kick each player had to sink to his knees to rebuild the little mound of dirt that was serving as a buttress, keeping the ball in place.

There's a certain camera angle that TV directors like to cut to during crucial penalty shoot-outs, capturing the view from immediately behind the taker. It may be an optical illusion but, framed in this way, the goal looks bloody huge. The players must hate this shot knowing that back at home, sinking deeper into or behind their sofas, the fans are already chuntering irritably about banjos and cows' arses. A word for the defence. There is a compelling body of evidence to suggest that, when the pressure is on, popping an immobile ball past a static keeper is not as easy as it looks. YouTube is awash with clips of delicate chips that become dreadful bobbling scuffs, but my personal favourite is locked away in a dusty memory vault. Early nineties, Spanish league game, Real Madrid. The culprit? Not quite sure: Butragueño? Possibly Hugo Sánchez? He places the ball, jogs forward, takes a terrific swipe, slicing across the very edge of the ball, and then watches in mounting horror as it arcs viciously away from goal, the crowds, the corner flag, finally coming to rest almost level with him on the touchline. If he had given it any more welly there's a real danger that it would have hit him on the back of the head.

Penalties, not so easy. Which made the beautifully calm, deft executions of the Darkies and Young Blues players all the more impressive. As for the conditions, remember Beckham's miss against Portugal in the Euro 2004 shoot-out? Hurling an accusatory glare at the pitch, trying to pin the blame for his ballooning skyrocket on a divot. David, sorry love, case dismissed. Try running into a howling gale lashing rain, grit and sand into your face to have a punt at a ball teetering on a little mound of mud.

With the scores deadlocked at 4-4 Young Blues' No14 stepped forward. Perhaps acknowledging his status in the team, a colleague accompanied him, fell prostrate at his feet and steadied the ball with an outstretched finger. The striker jogged forward and released a rocket that flew over the head of the Darkies' keeper and caught the centre of the crossbar. Tong. There was a stunned silence. The ball ricocheted almost to the edge of the centre circle; caught by a sudden gust of wind it gathered pace, cruising up the river of mud. If someone didn't retrieve it the first own-goal in penalty shoot-out history was on the cards. I trotted upfield and dribbled self-consciously back to the crowd scene, knocking a side-foot pass to the Darkies' last man, the tall, eloquent defender. He placed the ball with care on the small pile of dirt and turned to face the goal.

PATIENCE

As you climb to the highest point of Signal Hill, clambering aboard the lion's rump, Cape Town's possibilities spread before you. Table Mountain looms over the city bowl, a geometric slice of geology softened by the brilliant white cloth of cloud tumbling over it. As your eye follows the coastline from Indian to Atlantic, from False to Hout Bay the opportunities for sun, surf, sightseeing and shopping overwhelm the senses. At the meeting point of two oceans the candy-striped Green Point lighthouse gazes out to sea. In the far distance an island rises from the sparkling water, intriguing and remote, inviting visitors.

Forty years ago these same landmarks were recognisable; the difference was in their perception. Amidst the natural beauty drawn together around this sleek finger of land, man-made constructs like 'group areas' and 'reserved separate amenities' were quietly tearing the city apart. Back then, gazing across at Table Mountain the eye would settle in its foothills, on District 6; a ticking time-bomb for the authorities, a ticking clock for its residents. Viewed from afar, the tiny dots on the beaches were all part of a happy weekend crowd; up close the colour-coded seating arrangements told a different story.

When Basil D'Oliveira climbed to the summit of Signal Hill from his home on its slopes the view spoke not of possibilities but of despair. Looking down at the Green Point playing fields he saw the patchwork of pitches upon which his starring performances for the St Augustine's CC and Ariel's FC had won him his places in the South African national cricket and football teams – the non-white South African national cricket and football teams. Before long, non-white sport would be shooed off this land. Lifting his gaze out to sea, Basil could see the jagged outcrop of rocks lashed by the Atlantic that would soon become a chilling reminder of Apartheid's rage and iron grip. The year was 1959, it was time to escape.

Patience, charm and tenacity during a long correspondence with the legendary cricket journalist and broadcaster John Arlott earned D'Oliveira an invitation to try his luck in the Lancashire League. He never looked back. His first summer saw him lead Sobers at the head of the batting averages. Soon enough Worcestershire had signed him up. A pugnacious batsman, crafty swing bowler and athletic fielder, the only thing D'Oliveira dropped following his arrival was the four years he had spent waiting to escape. In 1966 the '30-year-old' received an England call-up. A month after Basil had made an impressive debut at Lord's – holding at bay a West Indian attack led by a rampant Wes Hall – another African wearing the colours of his adopted country took to the centre of London's sporting stage.

Born in what was then Maputo, Mozambique, Eusébio da Silva Ferreira was the star of the 1966 World Cup. Once Pelé had been hacked out of the tournament by the Portuguese defenders, their own 'black pearl' assumed his mantle. Hurst's hat-trick in the final will always be the highlight for English fans, but the trio that Eusébio stuck past the North Koreans remains the choice of the purist. Portugal were dead and buried at 0-3. A powerful runner with a jackhammer shot, Eusébio led the retaliatory charge. After slamming in his first two goals he trotted purposefully back to the halfway line, ball wedged under his armpit, eager for more. The third exemplified his style and power; a mazy run down the right flank, dart inside and exocet into the roof of the net. His fourth flew in from the spot after the tiring Korean defence had bundled him over midway through yet another surge at goal. The rematch 44 years later was the first game to be aired live in North Korea. It seems that after the seventh Portuguese goal flew in normal service was resumed as Korean Central Broadcasting returned to images of factory workers heaping praise on Kim Jong Il.

In the afterglow of the 1966 Wembley triumph, the national summer sport faded out of focus, but England's rally in a losing cause against the West Indies established Basil D'Oliveira as a man with a future. In another life it might have been him dashing across the turf at Wembley. If the African Football Confederation had not boycotted the tournament in protest at their limited allocation of places. If CAF had not expelled South Africa a decade earlier for refusing to send a racially-mixed team to the first African Nations Cup. If Fifa had not expelled FASA two years earlier for their failure to establish a truly representative body. If, if, if... To paraphrase a popular truism: if my auntie smoked a pipe she'd be my uncle. A superb all-round athlete, Basil's career was dogged with the ifs and buts spawned by the bitterly unhappy marriage of sport and politics. In the summer of 1968 it all kicked off.

It began with another English triumph at Wembley as Best, Charlton and Law led Manchester United to their first European Cup against Eusébio's Benfica. Again the Portuguese No10 carried away personal honour in the shape of the first European Golden Boot Award. A few months later, a few miles away in South London, Basil D'Oliveira scored a century that set South Africa on its path into the sporting wilderness. His 158 at the Oval was not critical in a sporting sense – the series was drawn, the Australians retained the Ashes. (Decades later another South African, Kevin Pietersen, scored the same number of runs at the same venue against the same opponents with markedly different results. Different men, different lives, a different world.) D'Oliveira's hundred in the summer of 1968 should have secured his berth for that winter's tour, but the destination was South Africa and his selection carried weighty diplomatic baggage. Cricketers play the game in whites, and at that time in South Africa this dress code extended to the skin of the national team – Apartheid laws decreed that white and coloured players could not share the same pitch. The MCC dithered messily, the governments of the two countries rattled covert diplomacies back and forth. When D'Oliveira's place in the touring party was finally confirmed, Prime Minister BJ Vorster chose to interpret this as a political slight and the tour was cancelled. It would be 30-odd years before English cricketers re-entered South Africa without the tag 'rebel' dangling about their necks.

Standing on top of Signal Hill, looking out across the endless oceans, I could see the brow of another hill, cut off from the mainland in past millennia, bubbling up from the frothing Atlantic surf a few miles off the coastline. Seal Island has the sort of jolly ring that might inspire Pixar to create a CGI fantasy in which a colony of sleek, oily mammals averts a man-made ecological disaster while exchanging snappy one-liners. Whisper its Dutch name and the fun stops: Robben Island. Even to those with a limited knowledge of South African history these words echo with a sombre resonance. In the Nelson Mandela Bay Stadium I watched a group of Brazilian fans taunting their Dutch counterparts with a banner that read "There's only one Robben and it's an Island". The scores of tiny orange specks I could see far below me marching towards the city centre heading for the semi-final had enjoyed the last laugh.

Made infamous by Nelson Mandela's incarceration in the early sixties, the Island established its status as a dumping ground for political prisoners in the 19th century when the British government deposited Xhosa chief Makana Nxele there following bloody skirmishes around the Grahamstown garrison. Mandela's approach was more subtle – the guerrilla tactics of Umkhonto we Sizwe were aimed at sabotaging the system, not taking lives, but the response of the ruling class was the same. From his place in the dock during the Rivonia trials Mandela calmly, eloquently laid out his beliefs – equality, freedom, inclusivity. Everything that Apartheid abhorred. Makana had surrendered to the British to save his people from further suffering; Mandela also made clear that he was prepared to die for his cause. I would guess that a government trying to control a society by enforcing a meticulously contrived dogma fears rational, principled, selfless opponents far more than the bug-eyed nutcake running towards them clutching a fizzing black orb screaming: "Die imperialist scum!" Mandela, like Makana, had to be tucked away out of sight, out of mind. A former leper colony, Robben Island housed some of the worst criminals flushed out of the Cape Town sewers. The political leaders – the real danger men – were put in solitary confinement.

Faced with the tedium of incarceration, a little sport goes a long way. *The Great Escape* opens and closes with Steve McQueen in 'the Cooler', drilling a baseball against the wall into his catcher's mitt. Kerthunk, thwock; kerthunk, thwock. On Robben Island the prisoners had soon fashioned makeshift footballs from tied up rags and were having kickabouts in their cells. Apart from their back-breaking shifts breaking stones in the lime quarry, a perfunctory tramp around the exercise square was their only other physical activity.

In December 1964 a respectful plea for a football was made to the governor, Captain Theron. A thoughtful man, he weighed the request with care. In December 1967 he agreed to half an hour on Saturday mornings. Despite their meagre diet and ragged clothing the Robben Island inmates had one resource in abundance: patience.

The first match was a casual affair, a celebration: two makeshift teams – Rangers v Bucks – watched by a small crowd, everyone involved savouring an exotic taste of their former lives. Having won the right to play, the men drew from their other great store: organisation. Isolated from family and the rest of the world they clustered around the embers of enthusiasm fired by this first game. From this tiny seed of normality a forest grew, spreading its shade across the unwilling inhabitants of the sun-bleached rock. Seven clubs formed under the banner of the Matyeni ('stones') Football Association, each with three teams (A, B and C) to allow everyone irrespective of age or ability to join in. This ethos of inclusivity extended further when a new team, Manong Rangers, joined the league, uniquely permitting membership from both the ANC and PAC – the two leading bodies of political dissent, battling a common foe back on the mainland, but ideologically divided.

Considering the conditions under which they operated, the level of organisation underpinning the league was staggering. Clubs corresponded formally between each other discussing transfers, disciplinary panels heard appeals, referees were trained in the laws of the game, meticulous fitness regimes were established.

Someone unearthed a copy of the Fifa rulebook amongst the sparse collection in the prison library. The Matyeni FA was reborn as the Makana FA, a constitution was drawn up, rules and order were applied. Thanks to the intercessions of the Red Cross, living conditions on the Island had gradually improved; food became more plentiful and varied, clothing arrived better suited to the vicissitudes of the Robben Island climate. Now football boots arrived – a ragtag assortment but a step forward from the heavy work boots the players had been wearing – and kit for each of the clubs; players and fans now had their true colours. Football's cultural elements also emerged with betting and bragging during the week leading up to Saturday fixtures. Teammates even managed to 'camp' together before the game, thanks to some deft footwork as they lined up to be filed into their cellblocks.

Appropriately Manong Rangers, the team that had side-stepped political differences, won the inaugural league, losing only one game all season. They received a small wooden shield that was promptly confiscated by the warders. Despite this flexing of authoritarian muscle, football was dragging the guards through a reverse Stockholm syndrome into closer union with the men they had been taught to fear and revile. They started to watch the game instead of the crowds, identified favourite players and formed covert allegiances to certain teams.

The following season as Manong were running away with the

league again, the Makana FA decided to freshen things up. A cup competition was launched with teams drawn from the 'regions' – each cell block. Ironically this only created an even more dominant force – Block C4 housed the finest players on the Island and they now came together as Atlantic Raiders.

The first round of the FA Cup glories in its own peculiar vernacular. There is mysticism (magic and romance), a dash of biblical symbolism (giant-killing) and some existential quandaries – can one really slip on a *potential* banana skin? The Makana FA Cup was no different. The opening fixture pitted the red-hot favourites Atlantic Raiders, against no-hopers – minnows, if you like – Blue Rocks. Against expectation, the run of play and stretched odds, the underdogs took an early lead. As the Atlantic Raiders poured forward in offensive waves the Rocks packed themselves into a wall of defence. At first it was funny, but as the crowd sensed an upset, tempers frayed. Eventually the embattled referee stormed from the pitch. A replacement was hastily summoned; the game ended without further score.

The Raiders' defeat bruised egos and wounded pride. A couple of days after the game the Makana FA received a letter from Raiders, complaining about the actions of the original official, invoking the Fifa rulebook. The contretemps gradually became a crisis. During a subsequent game disgruntled players staged a lying-down protest – disciplinary hearings were called, appeals lodged; copious correspondence flashed between the various protagonists, reams of precious paper were expended. Eventually a settlement of sorts was reached, but the 1970 season was lost. Even to this day many of the leading figures view the Atlantic Raiders episode as a low point for the Makana FA. It did however affirm the strength and integrity of this dispossessed group of men, rigid in their determination to play things by the book.

By the turn of the 1980s most of the men that had founded, forged and fought for the Makana FA had made their way back to the mainland. Looking back at the sprawl of rock fading into the horizon they would remember that Saturday morning in 1967 when they ran out onto the stony recreation ground, in prison boots and rags, to play football. They did not know then that 40 years after that first match they would return to the Island to see some of the world's finest players turn out for the Makana FA.

I WAS SITTING OUTSIDE A CAFÉ AT THE WATERFRONT SIPPING A coffee, surrounded by the hallmarks of modern, affluent South Africa. The Waterfront is the kind of place where scatter cushions reflect "lifestyle choices" and lampshades provide "lighting solutions". Further down the boardwalk a young busker with gently swaying dreadlocks was strumming his way through a lovely, slowed-down rendition of the Libertines song *A Time for Heroes*, which seemed apt given my destination that morning.

As Cape Town faded from view the powerful motors of the sleek, white dagger kicked in and we began to slice through the water. In decades past the crossing to the Island was made in a more ponderous fashion; the prisoners lurching and rolling in a darkened hold, bathed in fear and the bilious retchings of their colleagues.

At the quayside we were loaded into buses for a brief tour of the perimeter. The Island defied my preconception of an Alcatraz-style fortress; it was more like a village with a schoolhouse, church and mosque, the odd shop.

As our old bus rolled slowly over sandy roads between scrubby bushes, what struck me most powerfully about the place Oliver Tambo referred to as "Apartheid's least hospitable outpost" was the brightness. At ground level the odd imported eucalyptus tree and a few dusty bushes pass for greenery, but the dominant features are geomorphic: sand, rocks, stones – the Matyeni FA was aptly named. Looking at the dazzling limestone quarry where men had laboured for years, chivvied by shouts and the lash of sjamboks, I understood why many of them returned home with permanent eye damage. As we neared the main complex of prison buildings our guide pointed to some rocky slopes falling away to the sea, "and this was the warders' golf course".

"Their fucking *what?*" I heard myself mutter, raising a nervous eyebrow on the burly Canadian lady next to me.

I squinted at the scatter of stones and parched bushes and sighed. Wherever humanity is to be found waddling about bloated with its own self-importance, prancing around in self-imposed clownish attire, rigidly defending the needs of the few over the many, here you will find someone eagerly swishing a golf bat.

We arrived at the main prison complex and were met by our guide – a former inmate whose glasses and thickset frame leant him a striking resemblance to a man who had marshalled the Manong Rangers midfield during the early years of the Makana FA: Jacob Zuma. While our group gathered – chattering and fidgeting – he said nothing, just stood there, hands clasped before him, head bowed, swaying from one foot to the other, waiting for silence. Patience: more an art-form than a virtue for the inmates of Robben Island. His voice was worth the wait, a deep sonorous boom that rolled through the cool white corridors, bouncing off the thick walls. He led us into a dormitory, a small rectangle full of metal bunks – before the Red Cross intervened in 1978 the men laid mats on the floor – on which coarse, grey blankets sat neatly folded. On the wall a sheet of typeface explained the rationing policy: mealies for Bantus; rice and samp for Indians and Coloureds; one ounce of jam or syrup for Indians and Coloureds; nothing for Bantus. This pernickety attempt to maintain and reinforce the separation doctrine was soon scuppered by the prisoners, gladly sharing what they had equally.

Outside the cell block a stretch of grey stones pocked with fibrous little bushes was gated at either end by a pair of wooden poles, yellow with black stripes, bleached by the sun. A forgotten football pitch. From here the shouts of the crowd had once drifted over to the solitary confinement block, seeping through the thick iron tubes lining the tiny windows, reaching the ears of a man welcomed onto the Island as 466/64. We were shown Mandela's cell, still containing the simple rudiments of his life there – a small stool bearing a cup and plate, a bucket. I was in South Africa on New Year's Eve 1999 and watched soundless, deeply moving TV pictures of the former president returning to this tiny box, carrying a single candle.

Back on the mainland I headed for the Grand Parade. The square was a sea of orange as waves of Dutch fans flooded in through the gates. There was the crew of the Flying Dutchman in their peaked caps, aviator shades and lurid tangerine airline uniforms – easyJet on acid. There were guys riding ostriches wearing pith helmets; there were inflatable crowns and afro wigs, feather boas and clogs – real live clogsh! – and endless gangs in orange boiler suits, looking like the happiest death row in history. Up on the stage the cheerleader for the Oranje Supporters' Club bellowed to the crowd in between the songs booming from the speakers. Alongside *Ke Nako* and *Waka Waka* there was plenty of brassy oompah, oompah to stomp along to, and then the Queen back catalogue was plundered: a boozy chorus of *We Are The Champions* was soon followed by You Never Can Beat The Dutch, chanted over the bassline of *Another One Bites The Dust*. Beer flowed, smoke billowed, the sun shone – if it wasn't for Table Mountain looming in the background you would have sworn we were gathered in Amsterdam's Museum Square. A man wandered past in lavish 19th-century garb, dressed up as Jan van Riebeeck. The Mother City seemed to have embraced this fresh Dutch invasion with open arms, swiftly adopting yet another 'home nation'. The MC led a new round of chants – "Oranje! Oranje!" – the volume crept up to 11, the crowd was a giant tangerine, swollen with excitement, ready to burst open. I glanced up at the clock tower above City Hall. Only another four and a half hours until kick-off.

Gradually the amber army began to march, pouring out of the square into the surrounding streets. As the sun began to dip into the ocean behind us I let myself go with the flow, along Long Street's grand Victorian and Cape Dutch houses with their broad balconies and curving gables, finally washing up in another crowd gathering in Waterkant Street. Here, the mass of bodies was edging slowly forward towards a bridge in the distance that signalled the start of the Fan Walk. Building on the Fan Park idea developed for Germany 2006, the fan walks in South Africa were a brilliant but simple concept. A long meander to the stadium accompanied by food and drink, musicians and dancers, it meant that everyone could join the final march to the game, whether they had a ticket or not. The orange tide was ebbing slowly towards the bridge inch by inch. Up ahead a young man wearing enormous plastic glasses, a false nose and a shaggy orange clown wig bounced up on someone's shoulders: "Patience, patience – we're getting there, we're going all the way! Hup Holland Hup!"

I crossed the bridge, glanced back at the thousands still creeping towards it, then descended on the other side, dropping down into another world. I found myself in a clearing set amongst trees strung with multi-coloured lanterns in which a magical twilight carnival was in full swing. Open fires sent smoke drifting across the crowds; towering marionettes with giant gurning faces loomed from the shadows – a foretaste of Rio in 2014. There was even a giant Madiba beaming beatifically in full Bafana kit. Stilt-walkers in lavish costumes tottered about – one grinning Medusa had half a dozen vuvuzelas sprouting from her head. What struck me most was the seamless interweaving of diverse elements of South African cultures: the gumboot dancers from the northern mines, the minstrels from the Cape, the white farm stalls – "local is lekker " – serving up boerewors and melk tert. A group of Uruguayan fans walked past rather sheepishly and a raucous cheer swept through the crowd. The baddies, the team reviled after the Ghana game, had plunged to a sufficient depth of unpopularity that their handful of supporters were now hailed as heroes. World Cup 2010 loved the underdog. Walking through this bubbling cultural melting pot, part of a happy cosmopolitan crowd of locals and visitors, I felt, perhaps more than at any other time, the scale of the host nation's achievement. A Cape Minstrel walked past grinning and doffed his boater. Hats off to South Africa – in memorable scenes and wonderful moments like these they gave us a World Cup like no other.

The procession continued along Somerset Road cheered on by hordes of children lining the high walls on either side: a fanfare blared through vuvuzelas of all colours, and the subtle variations for the connoisseur: the curly kuduzelas and the tiny, squeaky kazoos – the babazelas. I drifted off to the side and wandered into a bar called Cubana. The fireglow bulbs lighting the interior camouflaged the orange hordes packed into every spare inch: rivers of Amstel flowed, chased down with trays of shots.

For the final leg of the journey, with the stadium rising like a spaceship in the night ahead of us, I walked with superheroes. They were the Superfans – a group of elderly gents in scarlet capes and red mining hard hats. And then there was a commotion behind me as a nondescript middle-aged man slipped through a gap in the fence to join friends on the other side. "Eh! Joel! Joel! That was Joel Stransky, did you see, it was Joel Stransky!" A man that, 15 years earlier, had kicked the ball that lifted South Africa to the top of the world after a long wait in the sporting wilderness.

Having read the story of the Robben Island league in Chuck Korr and Marvin Close's excellent book *More than Just a Game*, I wanted to hear a first-hand account from one of the key players. I drove over to Rondebosch Common to the Children's

Resource Centre and was greeted warmly at the door by a sprightly, bespectacled, grey-haired man, dressed all in white; a bundle of energy and enthusiasm. This was Marcus Solomon, one of the founders of the Makana FA.

Marcus showed me into a long room set out like a classroom with brightly-coloured plastic furniture and posters and photographic collages on the walls showing young people engaged in various sporting and cultural activities. There were slogans rejecting bullying and other anti-social behaviours; one that particularly caught my eye stated: "Every community must take charge of its own destiny." I asked Marcus how football had found its way onto Robben Island.

"We were interested in socialism, in how to react and behave in a space with other people. We knew all about the world we had left behind and wanted to see if we could create something new out there on the Island. We had a vision of a free South Africa that was all about inclusivity and doing away with these obsessions around separating and distinguishing people; we knew that these ideas had no long-term future.

"Sport is about learning how to deal with other people on a level field, playing by an agreed set of rules. We started playing chess, making the pieces from scraps of paper, but the warders found these and destroyed them. A lot of the guys were keen on soccer and soon we had a decision to make: should we continue to press for the right to play even if this means punishment, reduced food rations and so on. We agreed our course and stuck to it. I had always been more of a rugby player but I could see that soccer would unite the greater number and unlike chess it is a contact sport; when you're bouncing off people you have to learn how to deal with them and they with you.

"I was firmly of the view that we needed to do things properly. Organise ourselves according to the rules, show how we could rise above our surroundings. We had teams, committees and associations. Soon I was immersed in soccer: playing, coaching, refereeing, organising the officials' association; I was also the vice-president of Hotspurs. I think we were all proud of what we had created – from nothing we had a fully working soccer league. In these abnormal circumstances we had somehow created a world of normality. It might seem like we were living out a fantasy, but it was real and important. Everyone got involved – if you didn't play, you reffed or coached or maybe just supported. It brought the prisoners together in a positive way and because we had established the ground rules, we had the basis for respect. I once had to send off Steve Tshwete – he went on to become the sports minister in the first unified government. He didn't want to go, but you have to respect the game.

"Of course, as things developed, there was some conflict between playing for the love of the game and playing to win. There's a balance somewhere in the middle that's not always so easy to find. For sure there were some ups and downs, but ultimately there was unity; we always signed off our letters 'yours in sports'."

I asked Marcus how he saw the world of South African sport now.

"We hear a lot about transformation but I don't see so many black faces in the rugby and cricket teams. This business with enforcing quotas is all nonsense, you need to get things right at the grass roots; develop the facilities for young people and create the right kind of social environment – inclusive and unthreatening – so they feel welcome and energised. South Africa must use this great natural resource."

"Do you think 2010 will help?" I asked.

"Maybe I'm not the best person to ask about 2010. So much money has been poured into that new stadium – do they really need this in Green Point? I would like to see some of this effort and resource directed towards the children in the townships, then we could say that the event has a true legacy."

I asked Marcus where he thought I might find the heart of South African football. He leant across the table and drew some figures on my pad.

"Look, there are 46 million people in this country, right? Twenty million are children. Let's say ten million boys and ten million girls." He drew a circle around the last two numbers, emphasising the point with a dot from the nib of the pen. "Here is where our focus should be. We have a saying, 'The future is now'. We realised that on Robben Island – our destiny lay in our own hands: we could sit around or take control. It is the same for our young people, now is the time to support them for the future good of this country."

Bright-eyed, energetic, totally plausible, Marcus could have sold me a car with no wheels. Probably two. I'd seen conviction and enthusiasm like this before with Nelly – it was inspirational, irresistible.

The final fixture staged by the Makana FA was a rather one-sided affair; it finished 89-0. As part of the festivities marking the start of Mandela's 90th year a delegation including Marcus, other founding Makana members and a few other useful players – Eto'o, Gullit, Weah – headed for the Island for one last kickabout. Together they lined up before an empty goal to take a symbolic 89 shots at racism. At the end of the ceremony Fifa awarded the Makana FA honorary membership.

This gesture of recognition marked the end of a long road for South Africa's turbulent relationship with the world's sporting establishment. Although CAF had led the way by expelling the all-white football team from the African Nations Cup in 1957, the guardians of the global game took a little longer to act. SASF – the federation representing some 46,000 non-white players – were refused entry to Fifa due to gaps in their membership; perversely the 20,000 members of the whites-only FASA were accepted. This messy fudge came unstuck in 1961 when Fifa kicked them out, but returned two years later when Sir Stanley Rous, the English president of Fifa, reversed the decision. A year later in 1964 they were kicked out again but it was only in 1976 that Fifa passed a formal resolution excluding South Africa while Apartheid existed. A decade earlier the IOC had voted to maintain South Africa's exclusion from the Olympics while they continued a long debate over their eligibility. A glance at their own charter might have saved some time: "Any form of discrimination with regard to a country or a person on grounds of race, religion, politics, gender or otherwise is incompatible with belonging to the Olympic Movement." In the end the threat of boycotts from other nations ahead of the 1968 Games in Mexico City brought matters to a head. Apartheid South Africa had no place at a Games that provided one of the defining images in the history of sporting politics: American sprinters Tommie Smith and John Carlos atop the medal rostrum, heads bowed, their black-gloved fists raised in salute.

International rugby was the last to go. The jewel in the sporting crown of white South Africa – a powerful symbol of Afrikaner identity: conservatism, strength, control and order, hallmarks of the Apartheid establishment – was hardest to pry out thanks largely to the company it kept. The key players in the IRB were predominantly white nations. The main dissent came from New Zealand (a country wrestling with its own dark past) and was traceable back to the exclusion of George Nepia – one of the greatest All Blacks of all time – from the all-white 1929 tour to South Africa.

Even after formal ties were severed, the promise of riches led international sportsmen back to the forbidden land. Many of the star names that claimed the inaugural Rugby World Cup for the All Blacks in 1987 had toured South Africa a year earlier in the guise of 'the Cavaliers'. At the turn of the nineties Mike Gatting's ill-fated cricket tour muddied the waters as Mandela's release date approached.

Now, almost two decades after South Africa began to emerge slowly out of the sporting wilderness, they were preparing to stage the biggest match in the world. If one had to sum up the semi-finals in a single phrase it would probably be: good things come to those who wait. The veterans Puyol and Van Bronckhorst scored fantastic goals to set up a final between two great footballing nations that had often fallen short in past tournaments. The first African World Cup was guaranteed the rare prize of crowning a new nation as champion – a satisfying outcome for the hosts and Fifa.

Out on Robben Island the peeling paint of the striped posts at either end of the pitch outside D Block had reminded me of the rainbow goalposts I had seen in the Transkei. In both locations football offered an escape. The young boys trying to plant one between the stripy sticks in the rural wilds were running out at the Bernabéu, Camp Nou, Old Trafford, becoming Kaká, Messi, Rooney. Although Chief Makana failed in his bid to escape the Island – drowning in the treacherous sea – every Saturday the men that played football under his name succeeded, running for their lives, over the fences, past the guards and dogs and across the water. They kept going until they reached the Green Point Track, Curries Fountain, the Orlando Stadium. There they could become the great players they had left behind – Mokone, Stadig, Sono, Motaung – ageless heroes, frozen in time.

For me the beauty, the subtle genius, of the Makana League lay not on the stony pitch but in the prison library. Fate saw men treated like dogs and threw them a bone; they swallowed it whole. Fifa's fastidious little tome was seized upon, pored over. It became the bible of their new religion as football fever swept through the cellblocks; a welcome diversion, a source of hope. It's a wonderful irony that men denied their liberty by the controlling neurosis of Apartheid found redemption in a complex of regulations, a set of rules established by a higher authority, an authority that had already lost patience with football on the mainland and cut it adrift.

WHATEVER HAPPENED TO
THE DANGEROUS DARKIES?
(PART 2)

EARLY ONE MORNING, ABOUT A YEAR BEFORE JOHANNESBURG hosted the opening scenes of the 2010 World Cup story, I was driving up Constitution Hill skirting the border between Hillbrow and Braamfontein – two of the city's more notorious suburbs – heading for the Old Fort. A former residence of Mahatma Gandhi and Nelson Mandela, the Fort is now used for more civilised purposes than entombing political dissidents. A large rectangular complex of ramparts and gables, its brilliant white stucco walls radiated the lucid morning sunshine – it looked like the kind of place Clint Eastwood would hole up in, ready for the blazing, bloody denouement of a Sergio Leone film. That morning the courtyards were buzzing with industry as members of the Forum for the Empowerment of Women (FEW) arrived for their annual general meeting. After a few enquiries I found the person I had come to see, Phumla Rose Masuku. Phumla's role at FEW was to run projects that used sport and the arts to reach out to gay women marginalised by the homophobic elements of township life. There was a small coffee shop at the back of the Fort, overlooking a stony parade ground bleached white by decades of unrelenting sun. Once two tall glasses of icy Fanta had arrived, I asked Phumla to tell me about The Chosen Few.

She was a slight, skinny figure peering out from beneath the brim of an oversized baseball cap, but when she smiled I recognised the same combination of mischief and steely determination that I had seen in Nelly, Marcus and many others committed to using football as a positive force in South Africa.

"It started when we were running some courses – computer skills, photography, that sort of thing – and, during the break one day I got my football out. I've loved soccer all my life, my ball is always in my bag. So we had a kickaround. I was captain and founder of the first township team – Soweto Ladies – but even there you got discrimination; some players felt threatened, there were some homophobic elements. In the end we decided to create a space of our own to enjoy the game; we became The Chosen Few. At first we played some local boys' teams and soon realised that we could take on whoever we liked.

"Most of our players had been victims of hate crimes, their confidence had been damaged – now we had faith in our own team – now, we were so out. Soon we had more than thirty players – all we needed was a real challenge. So we set our sights on the Gay Games in Chicago. Somehow we managed to scrape together enough money to take a team to the Games. For us, just being there was a beautiful experience – it proved that we could represent ourselves, our country, on a bigger stage."

"How did you get on in the tournament?" I asked.

Phumla beamed. "Hey, not so bad, we came third – I thought we would make the final but we came up against some pretty tough opponents in our semi - eeh, those girls were rough, man."

I looked across the table at this township scrapper, a woman who had clearly spent most of her life facing difficult challenges head on.

"Who were you playing?" I asked, taking a sip from my Fanta.

"Hackney Ladies."

I choked for a while, then snorted for dear life, inflating a fizzy orange bubble in my left nostril.

"So, what is the next challenge?" I asked, reaching for a napkin.

"Well, the next Games are in Cologne in 2010 – we want to be there, and this time we will win it."

"And what about the tournament taking place over here that summer?"

"Ag man, that World Cup is just about the money; they're not interested in the likes of us. But hey, who is the most successful team? The Soccer Queens collected a bronze medal at our Games – when did Bafana last do that? For 2010 it's all about SAFA, Fifa and the teams from overseas. What will it do for us in the township? They don't even come there to look for workers for the stadium – it's all the same old corporations. Why not share it out? Give fish to some and bread to others."

"Where do you think the heart of South African football lies?" I asked.

"Eh, that's a tough one. This game really all revolves around men, but did you know that Kaizer Motaung's mother was a soccer player? That's where he gets his game from. For me, it's in my heart – always has been – I was born loving this game. Now when I see these girls who have come through some nasty times, running around the pitch, scoring goals, winning games and medals – they have pride, they are out there, they are the heart of what soccer means to me."

I thought of The Chosen Few often over the following months as the tournament coasted towards South Africa, building an unstoppable wave of excitement and anxiety, hope and fear. I could understand Phumla's scepticism about the longer-term benefits of the World Cup, but what was more surprising was the entrenched cynicism in other quarters questioning South Africa's ability to deliver it at all. Even as the opening match drew near many seemed convinced that a fiasco was on the cards: unfinished stadia, incompetent administration, unchecked crime. But when the tournament finally arrived, flooding across the country, the prophets of doom were washed away. A decade into the 21st century, over four short weeks, South Africa put on a wonderful show.

The spirit of the Spanish champions seemed to exemplify the ethos underlying the efforts of the host nation: a unified group that valued collective endeavour above individual glory. Who better to score the decisive final goal than Iniesta – the 'anti-galactico'? Here was a nation that for many years had bounced between over-inflated expectation and saggy disappointment – their blueprint for success should be pored over by others with a similar problem. It would be easy now to claim that I always suspected England would fall short, but that would be dishonest – heading into the tournament I willingly clambered aboard the overcrowded bandwagon. And why not? Part of the fun of a World Cup is casting aside the cynical world of adulthood to rediscover the childish joy of unconditional optimism. In a tournament where pragmatism and professionalism narrowed the gap between the thoroughbreds and the workhorses, I longed for Brazil to cut loose and prance to victory with dash and finesse. Watching them try to bully the Dutch in Port Elizabeth was a big let-down; Lubez, screaming his lungs halfway up his throat, drowned out the sound of my ten-year-old self, shouting a running commentary around the garden, convinced I was Sócrates.

Of course the toughest challenges for the 2010 World Cup were not on the pitch. The real issue was always going to be what happened after the trophy had been lifted and the crowds had turned away. You could feel the hangover in South Africa on July 12 – an end to communal distractions at work; the specially extended school holiday was over – a Monday morning *babalas* like no other. The government needed clear heads to wade through the swamps of statistics and figures. The Finance Ministry estimated a R38bn boost to the economy thanks to the World Cup, and the creation of 130,000 new jobs. The tourism industry had welcomed an estimated 400,000 visitors and hoped many would come again and tell their friends. But it was never going to be possible to measure the success of this World Cup simply by crunching numbers.

Writing in the South African *Sunday Times* as the tournament entered its second week, the Local Organising Committee CEO Danny Jordaan sketched out the bigger picture: "This World Cup has created a platform for South Africans to interact with the world, but also with themselves." A week earlier under the headline "Afrikaners is plesierig oor sokker" *Die Burger* reported that over 340,000 Afrikaans-speakers had tuned in to Supersport to watch Bafana Bafana play Mexico – well over half the number that had watched the Super 14 rugby final. Grabbing someone's attention is easy enough, but it's another thing holding it. It was noticeable that the day before the World Cup Final, coverage of the opening Tri-nations fixture between the Springboks and New Zealand was starting to edge football off the back pages.

In any event I suspect Jordaan had more than just sporting integration in mind. When I caught the train from Cape Town to the suburb of Observatory after the first semi-final, there was a party atmosphere in the packed carriage. As they blew their vuvuzelas and waved their flags the predominantly white, middle-class locals chattered excitedly, not just about their sudden plunge into the world of "soccer" but the fact that they had abandoned their cars and were riding the battered old Metro. When we stopped for a few minutes at the station in Woodstock one wag suggested that the wheels had been stolen, another argued that the copper had been lifted from the overhead lines. Humour masking the serious problems associated with Cape Town's rich/poor divide. Rattling home through the darkness of the no-go areas was a bit of fun, a novelty; but further out of town in Khayelitsha the reality of life in such places that night was a candle tumbling to the floor of a wooden shack, creating a raging blaze that left nine dead. It may sound like a trite observation from an outsider who has merely scraped his fingernail over the uneven contours of South African life, but I'll say it anyway. If the wealth generated by the World Cup could contribute in some way to dragging those on the fringes of

South African society a little closer to a better life, then it would have achieved something that many identified as its primary goal.

So what did happen to the Dangerous Darkies? We left the eloquent defender in Lawaai Kamp, facing his penalty. He placed the ball with care on the small pile of dirt and turned to face the goal. As he did so the match on the neighbouring pitch came to a noisy end and the players and spectators drifted over to join us. In the far distance I could see the thick, spreading base of the Outeniqua Mountains, their ridges and peaks obscured by a leaden curtain of cloud. Beyond them towards the sea, I spotted the stretch of blue sky running along the coast that had convinced me to leave home that morning in shorts and a T-shirt. As the wind whipped up goosebumps on my bare arms and legs I looked over at the row of guys in hats and warm coats tucked snugly along the length of a low cement wall, passing long drooping cigarettes from hand to hand. I leant back against a wire fence which gave and juddered, swaying in the wind, reminding me of the afternoon resting against the shuddering water pipe at the old Oppenheimer Stadium in Orkney. What had I learnt since then?

In a sports-mad country football speaks eloquently of a divided society. It is South Africa's most popular game but only in a literal sense; a pastime for the masses, 'their game'. We are familiar with the idea of class separating sporting preferences – before Gazza's tears, *Fever Pitch*, Posh and Becks, before the Premiership laid on the prawn sandwiches, the English game clung to working-class roots. The difference in South Africa, as it tries to outrun its sad history, is that class and race are entwined and quite noticeably tied up in sport. Quoted in the 1958 Race Relations survey, Minister of the Interior Theophilus Dönges set out Apartheid's stall: "Whites and non-whites should organise their sporting activities separately, there should be no inter-racial competitions within South Africa, the mixing of races in teams should be avoided, and sportsmen from other countries should respect South Africa's customs and she respect theirs."

Even today it still seems like the historically 'white sports' rugby and cricket – the twin pillars of the Republic's international success – cast patronising glances in the direction of football. Some harmless fun for those needing a tribal banner to gather under – witness the mindless devotion to Chiefs and Pirates; a parochial obsession with little significance in the wider world. A mismanaged sport beset by innuendo and sleaze. Even within the traditional football communities the young guys have turned their heads for other reasons – gazing up at the global icons, galacticos from another planet.

I eased back on to the fence just as a light rain began to fall and reflected on the brighter side of South African football. Leaving a game to the masses may not be such a bad thing; R20 for a PSL ticket at least keeps it within the reach of its fans. For more than a decade, following a club in the English top flight has required deep pockets. The easy-going accessibility to the PSL clearly helps to create the relaxed atmosphere I found at league matches. The vuvuzelas, singing and dancing were more carnival than concentration. Of course the fans want their side to win, but there wasn't the nasty edge when things went wrong, the invective poured on opposing players and officials. I would suggest that, in South Africa, the game doesn't take itself too seriously. The mock riot at Orkney tickled the light-hearted underbelly of the fiercest rivalry in domestic football. When an angry mob gathered on the pitch at Celtic, the beefy drag queen leading the charge evoked more pantomime than pandemonium. It was good to watch football in this kind of environment, it was effortlessly enjoyable.

And then there's the style issue. The criticisms crop up in various forms: style over substance; too much showboating, too many tricks; the game is immature. Does good football have to be grown up? Will you really win nothing with kids? As pundits go I'd choose Picasso over Hansen: "Every child is an artist. The problem is how to remain an artist once we grow up."

In my school playground we wanted to be Hoddle, not Robson, and some of us had the mullets to prove it. We chose the fantasy of the spiralling, goal-bound 30-yard lob over the grim reality of tireless midfield endeavour. The South African fans are no different. They cling to their Aces and Doctors – their playground superstars – wrapping them in mythologies, urging them to produce the party pieces, the crowd-pleasers. Are the fans aiming too low or simply recalibrating their expectations? Either way they're not alone. What do fans of the vast majority of English Premiership clubs really hope for? A final league position somewhere between 5th and 17th. The pressure is on to keep the fingernails embedded in the flesh of the cash cow. Winning ugly? Not a problem. A dour 0-0 between Blackburn and Bolton that keeps them both tucked safely in mid-table for another week? Yes please.

Actually, no thanks. So a football culture that clings to mythologies and adores gratuitous skill is immature. Fine. Better than a studious devotion to results over pleasure. The average South African fan lives in abject poverty, R20 buys an afternoon of fun and escapism – put a price on that.

The noise from the crowd of players and spectators gradually subsided. The defender jogged forward slowly and caressed a shot just inside the right post. Ting. The keeper had no chance. As an idiot savant had pointed out at half-time, his girth demanded a shot to the extremities. The crowd surged on to the pitch, a chaos of bodies, singing and dancing in and out of dust clouds. In their midst the Darkies players, reformed into their huddle, were solid as a rock as the world around them swayed and billowed.

My mother-in-law tells a story from her childhood growing up in Mowbray on the less salubrious side of the train tracks running through Cape Town, concerning a paternity suit against a local man.

Advancing her case for maintenance payments, a young woman treated the court to an impassioned account of the relationship that she had shared with the man. Asked by the magistrate to explain what had happened the putative father paused, shrugged helplessly and said,

"Dit was net 'n blasie wind en 'n korrel sand." ("It was just a puff of wind, a grain of sand.")

In sport, as in life, it is often the fine margins that make all the difference between success and failure. Remember Gazza sliding into Germany's six-yard box in the dying stages of the Euro '96 semi-final, stretching every sinew of a surgically-scarred body, trying to graze the ball across his studs and into the unguarded net? He scores, England go on to win the final, ending 30 years of hurt; the scorer later retires to the golf course and after-dinner speaking circuit, a contented man. A few days before the World Cup he walked away from the wreckage of a car crash, the latest near miss in a life spiralling slowly into darkness. Back on the pitch, one of the most alluring sub-plots of the tournament, the African challenge, also stumbled into the chasm separating success and failure. If only Katlego Mphela's shots against Mexico and France had caught the inside of the woodwork, rather than the outside; but for the hand of Luis Suarez, Asamoah Gyan would not have even needed to take his penalty. As ever the deserted playing field is littered with ifs and buts. What went wrong? A few inches here, a micro-second there. A puff of wind, a grain of sand.

A few centimetres to the left and that last penalty would have caught the post flush – more tang than ting – sending the result, and the Darkies, in a different direction. But somehow the ball had found its way from a little pile of grit and sand through the howling gale and across the goal-line. My final hope for the 2010 World Cup is that it travels well, spreading the best of the world's biggest sporting event far and wide, right across the map of South Africa. When the opening game kicked off at Soccer City, Jabulani glided over fresh, lush turf; as it crossed the touchline the linesman's pristine flag fluttered. I would like to think that when next I visit Lawaai Kamp, to witness grass-roots development of the game, the wonderful, unbreakable spirit remains but the baked mud and milk bottles have been left far behind.

The pitches were soon deserted, only bovine life remained. A ragged specimen with crooked horns and a dirty hide matted by the rain sweeping across the fields trudged into a boggy goalmouth and nibbled the wisps of grass clinging to the penalty spot, before leaning its forehead against the foot of the post, nudging gently. I walked back into the township and found the car. The sudden warmth and silence as I pulled the door, shutting out the elements, felt indescribably luxurious. Around me the corrugated iron and tarpaulin of the shacks rattled and flapped in the driving wind. Across the rooftops, I spotted the tall match-winner heading for home, his arm draped around the shoulders of a much shorter teammate. Against the grey sky they looked bright and hopeful in their gold and black shirts, the silver lining from their manager's redundancy. In his free hand, another bright speck of colour, the white plastic milk bottle – a flag for the day – swung by his side. If football does have a heart I knew then that I was looking straight at it, watching it pulse with life.